Overcoming Evil

Biblical Spiritual Warfare Training Course
The complete eight lesson training course
from The Joseph Plan
an ebook

by Rev Thomas Holm

http://www.thejosephplan.org

Solid Christian Biblical Spiritual Warfare and Deliverance Training!

Overcoming Evil contains the complete eight lesson Biblical Spiritual Warfare and Deliverance Training course taught by The Joseph Plan. It, along with the course textbook, will arm you for spiritual warfare.

Christians from all over the world are now learning this vital element of the Christian Faith. It is available for church small group studies.

Warning! Warning! If you are not a Christian, you probably will be at the conclusion of this training.

In this training you will learn all the basic principles of spiritual warfare. It will prepare you for the spiritual battles of today and the ones to come.

Published by Rev Thomas Holm. 2014 The Joseph Plan

Edited by Jeanine Holm

Contents

Introduction: Training for Overcoming Evil!................................1

Lesson One: Basics of Becoming an Overcomer........................5

Lesson Two: Understanding the problem.................................15

Lesson Three: Obtaining the Authority over the enemy.................35

Lesson Four: Seek Righteousness, Gain Power.........................51

Lesson Five: Symptoms of Demonic Oppression.......................73

Lesson Six: Deliverance from all Demonic................................89

Lesson Seven: How and Why to Plead the Blood....................107

Lesson Eight: Putting it all into Action...................................119

Bonus Lesson: Self Deliverance..131

About the Author: Rev/Pastor Thomas Holm........................153

The World-Wide Ministry of The Joseph Plan

www.thejosephplan.org

Introduction
Training for Overcoming Evil!

An eight lesson training course

"OVERCOMING EVIL" contains the complete eight lesson training course as developed and distributed worldwide by The Joseph Plan.

Welcome to The Joseph Plan's Biblical Spiritual Warfare training series. A special teaching program offered by The Joseph Plan to all mature Christians desiring to become a mature Christian spiritual warrior.

If you are serious about learning or upgrading your knowledge about spiritual warfare this teaching is your answer.

The training consists of a series of lessons that are contained in this book. Each will pertain to different topics. We encourage you to study them one at a time. This is a level one, two and three training, so take what you need and leave the rest for when you are ready for it.

This study is biblically based, we do not teach new age or eastern spiritual philosophies. Everything contained in this teaching is rooted or directly taken from the Word of God. Our goal will be to give you the tools and biblical learning's to be free from the influences of the demonic and how to grow into being of service to other people.

We are all in a spiritual war today. Because of the age we are living in the power of the demonic is rising. Our problem is a lack of knowledge and the lack of teaching on the proper application of that knowledge. Much of modern churchianity avoids this vital topic. The God of creation, Jesus Christ, is powerful enough to overcome ALL!

Our study guide or teaching textbook is the "Biblical Spiritual Warfare Manual". I recommend you to get your own copy. It is available on Amazon Kindle or in our little Spiritual Warfare book store on the website and it is donation priced.

It is recommended that one studies these teachings with another Christian or a small study group if you can.

The lessons are presented in a particular order and it is strongly suggested that you study them one at a time and that you resolve any questions or issues that are raised before you go on to the next lesson. This is not a novel or short story to be read over one weekend. I encourage you to treat this teaching very seriously. Lookup all the references and pray continuously while in study.

The world is at war with everything that is Godly and righteous and you are being given the opportunity to put on the complete armor of God for the battle. Be diligent about this and I guarantee you your life will change. The Word of God contains the tools for you to be an Overcomer!

Get your bible, you are going to want to use it and you will be blessed when you do.

This type of solid bible study will benefit you the most if you:

Do one lesson at a time with another Christian or a small group if possible.

Look up each bible verse referenced in the bible.

Read and resource the "Biblical Spiritual Warfare Manual" during each lesson.

Pray before, during and after each lesson. God will lead you.

Prepare yourself to become the "Son (or daughter) of God" that He created you to be!

Commit yourself to that goal. Do all eight lessons. Be willing to allow yourself to change. Let God do for you what you cannot do for yourself. If you could do all this on your own, you most likely already would have. It is a new day and we are going to start it on lesson one! Are you committed? Get your bible.

The eight lessons should be studied and prayed individually. For the most powerful experience do this study with a small group.

Lesson One

Basics of Becoming an Overcomer

MAY WE START IN PRAYER!
Heavenly Father, In the name of our Lord and Savior, Jesus Christ, we come to you today and ask that you open and prepare our minds and hearts for the truths given to us through The Word! We humbly ask Father that you guide us and protect us during these times of study and learning. We desire to learn your ways Lord. Please help us. Please teach us. Help us to be willing and honest with ourselves. Help us to discern the truths contained in this teaching and to grow through them.

In Jesus Christ's name we ask.   Amen

God never promised us that being a Christian meant a life of no problems. Actually the Word of God tells us exactly the opposite. In John 16:33 it explains the world we live in.

John 16:33 These things I have spoken unto you, that in me ye might have peace. In the world ye shall have tribulation: but be of good cheer; I have overcome the world.

Through and because of Jesus we can find peace and overcome the evil. Tribulations that come from the world are one of our biggest problems. It manifests in institutions, other people and even in some family members. We all are exposed to it. Evil does exist.

Christians from all over the world have been writing The Joseph Plan, asking for answers. You are not alone. Asking questions like:

"Help me? I am tormented by evil thoughts and haven't slept for weeks..."

""Can someone help us? My two daughters and I are hearing voices and weird sounds in our house and are at wits end. Nothing that we have done has......"

"Pastor Thomas, I have developed very irrational fears and I am imagining all kinds of odd things. I am having nightmares that wake me up in a cold sweat. It is terrible!!!"

"It had gotten so severe in our apartment building that a vase came sailing across our living room and hit my husband in the back of his head. There was only he and myself in our home at the time. It almost scared him to death. Thank-you for all the Word inspired teachings on this vital subject. Our church never talks about it. I think they are scared to touch it. We wanted it all, so we bought your marvelous spiritual warfare book and are truly blessed. Now we both are taking our God given position over the demonic and finally finding peace. Thank-you Pastor."

These questions and many more are all covered in this teaching from The Joseph Plan. There are many teachings onsite and I offer the Biblical Spiritual Warfare Manual to all as your comprehensive companion study guide. It is our resource manual and textbook.

The Biblical Spiritual Warfare Manual is by far my most in depth and comprehensive attempt at sharing the information I have been taught and the experiences I have accumulated over the last twenty years about Spiritual

Warfare and Deliverance. It is the study guide for this teaching series

Let's get started.

The first key to overcoming the evil within or around oneself is coming to grips with the reality of the spirit world. God is SPIRIT. The Devil is SPIRIT. The Angels are SPIRIT, The Demons are SPIRIT. The spirit world is real, existing in a different dimension than the one we live in, but very real and active.

We need to understand that God, in His Word, says that Lucifer went into revolt as well as one third of all the angels and was kicked out of the heavenly dimension into ours.

We must make an admission to ourselves that they are real and possess certain powers. We need to accept the fact that some or probably many of the problems in our life are caused by these demonic entities, spirits or demons.

The second key is acknowledging within your innermost self that God IS and no other created being is higher or more powerful than Him. He and only He, has the power and the authority to take dominion and command over ALL members of the spiritual world.

If you belong to a church or group that understands and teaches this reality and has given you the tools to deal with it, you are blessed. The biggest problem in getting solid spiritual warfare teachings into the hands of the layman Christian is the lack of teaching that the demonic world and thus the spiritual powers are real and can be dealt with.

What a contrast between teaching and conducting spiritual warfare in America versus so many of the other countries of the world. There is a big contrast between teaching spiritual warfare in the USA and in overtly dark regions.

Most churches in America and thus many Christians do not recognize the reality and power of Satan today. They just don't get it that Satan has infiltrated so much of their lives, even within the church. There is very little formal spiritual warfare teaching and thus very little spiritual warfare practiced.

The situation in other areas or countries is quite different however. We are ministering worldwide. We have communicated by email recently to Christians in New Zealand and various countries in Africa and find a startling different problem there. There the demonic is horribly evident or obvious. It is very well understood who the enemy is. The primary problem is that many of these wonderful men of God, when they were called, picked up the bible and started a study and maybe a church, with very little actual training in spiritual warfare. There are isolated places with very good spiritual warfare teachings. But much needs to be done. These pastors are eager to find THE SOLUTION. They are keenly aware of who the enemy is.

The problem of teaching spiritual warfare is different from continent to continent and area to area. Below is a comparison chart I was sent that displays the differences.

AMERICA and other countries being deceived	KNOWN DARK COUNTRIES
IGNORANT, SKEPTICAL of demonic activity	AWARE, CONVINCED of demonic activity
Demonic LAST RESORT, if ever	Demonic ALWAYS CONSIDERED
USA founded in LIGHT, turning to DARKNESS	In past DARKNESS, now LIGHT coming
SUBTLE, HIDDEN work of Satan	OPEN, OBVIOUS work of Satan
CAMOUFLAGED activities, GRAY to hide it	OVERT EVIL evident, DARK clearly shown
Christians UNTRAINED, FEARFUL of demons	Christians, many are UNTRAINED but TRYING
Demons, Satan GROWING STRONGER	Demons, Satan slowly LOSING GROUND

A stark contrast! Most American denominational churches today are not teaching and equipping the saints for the battles we all face. They don't seem to realize that we are in a war or care that there is a tremendous need for spiritual warfare teaching. Many Christian brothers and sisters are being hurt because of the lack of solid teaching.

Gaining the proper knowledge and understanding that Satan is real and the need for Spiritual Warfare training is the first step in becoming an Overcomer. It doesn't matter what country you live in, we are all in need and should strive to learn what the Lord has given us to help us.

Satan's work in America is far more subtle than in many places. Few churches recognize and teach that Satan is real in America. Here Satan works behind the scenes and within the halls of the churches and the government. Satan works overtime in making sin and all its consequences "socially acceptable". Yet the outcome is the same as in countries where the demonic is more overt. The result is bondage, bondage to sin and all that it entails. In America Satan is actually more dangerous, because he has done much of his work in secret and has not been exposed. That is one difference between the USA and many other countries. In America (Babylon) today, sin rules and thus does not get treated as demonic. Like any disease, if it isn't recognized and diagnosed it is more dangerous than one whose symptoms are obvious and given the proper treatment.

No wonder so many are experiencing demonic oppression and attacks. Sneak attacks!

Paul says we should not be unaware of Satan's ways and traps (2 Corinthians 2:5-11). In this country most Christians don't recognize Satan's tactics and many don't even believe he exists and are not prepared to fight against him. In many parts of the world they know he exists and they know his evil ways and recognize him as the enemy. Recognizing evil is half the battle.

Satan's power is growing worldwide, because it is turning toward sin and further away from Jesus' ways. His power is growing in ways we could never have imagined.

Proverbs 14:34 Righteousness exalts a nation, but sin is a disgrace to any people.

Do you see sin increasing around you and righteousness fading? Do you see the demonic rising? There is a direct correlation between sin in and around us and the power of the demonic. Sin gives the demonic permission to operate and gives the demonic its strength.

As a nation, state or local community becomes tolerant of sin, the powers of the demonic increase. Allow sin into your life and the natural consequence is that you will be attacked and harassed by the demonic. You can even become physically sick. As society accepts sinful ways to become the norm, it is giving the demonic "legal permission to operate" and to "possess and use" its institutions and people. The Devil knows this and is taking every opportunity to take advantage of the situation. The opposite of sin is righteousness.

1John 2:1 My little children, these things write I unto you, that ye sin not. And if any man sin, we have an advocate with the Father, Jesus Christ the righteous:

When we repent of the sin in our life and are saved, we are given the gift of righteousness. Righteousness is the breastplate we need that protects us in any spiritual battle. It is part of the armor of God that He gives us so we can stand upright and use all the spiritual weapons at our disposal. Seven days a week.

Eph 6:14 Stand therefore, having your loins girt about with truth, and having on the breastplate of righteousness;

The breastplate of righteousness protects us from the flaming arrows of temptation that the enemy uses against us.

Our enemy is crafty. He comes against us in many different ways. He is always there, always hanging around, waiting for the opportune time to attack or use us for his purposes, which are never for the good. Remember the devil and all his minions (demons) hate the righteous and want to kill or destroy us. He is the source of all lies and is working full time to deceive and destroy your relationship with the Lord.

There are two primary battle fronts in spiritual warfare. Two battle lines that must both be addressed.

Whether your battle is with the <u>enemy around you</u> or the <u>enemy within</u>, there is help in God's Word. There are lessons we can all use to be Overcomers in this war for our souls and lives.

The first and most important is the battle front that lies within us, the war for our mind and soul. This battle is conducted through deliverance. We need to be delivered from the grips or attacks of the demonic and into the loving hands of Jesus. When we talk about deliverance it isn't just for people who are "possessed" with the devils demons. It is also the process for any Christian to free themselves from sinful thoughts or actions (sin) that may provide a demonic influence in their lives. Yes, a Christian can have a demon. Paul of the New Testament had a demon and if he did---so can we.

In order to be free of spiritual attacks or demonic oppression, we need to have Deliverance. Deliverance from the root causes of spiritual oppression. Deliverance is being set free, free from all that is oppressing you. One receives deliverance in a three stage process. You have to get involved and do all of the stages in order for it to be successful. If one skips any of them or can't be honest with themselves, deliverance will most likely not be successful. Spiritual Warfare most likely will fail if you aren't sincerely thorough.

The three primary stages of Deliverance are:

1. Identify and tear down the strongholds that have given the demonic permission.

2. Remove the legal rights that the demonic has acquired.

3. Cast out the demons to be set free.

Once these three stages are completed one must then fill the spiritual house that was just cleaned with the spirit of Jesus, the Holy Spirit. Repentance and Obedience are at the foundation and we discuss those in later chapters.

If you try to cast out a demon without first dealing with the reason it is affecting you in the first place, it will result in an unsuccessful deliverance. Removing the root sin (or curse) that is giving the demonic its authority is crucial to completing a successful deliverance. You may be able to temporarily remove the demon, but you will not have taken away the stronghold that allowed it to be there in the first place. I explain the process of discovering what your part is in being set free from demonic oppression in later chapters of this course and explicitly in the course manual.

The research, experience and learning's of some of the best Spiritual Warfare teachers are contained in the "Biblical Spiritual Warfare Manual. Review the introduction and chapter one with this lesson.

So where do we start?

This process has to start with our admission that we aren't God. But there is ONE and His name is Yeshua. That we aren't perfect and that only God, Jesus Christ is, for He is fully God and today sits in heaven, over all with the Father. Once we can make that confession we can accept that we are, by our inner nature, a sinner. Sin is the root of our spiritual problems. Especially willful sins, acts or behaviors that we choose to do in spite of God's will for us. Willful, repetitive, unrepentant sin gives the demonic special permission to establish a stronghold in our body and mind from which they can have a very powerful place to operate from.

The second battle front that we are all soldiers of is in the outside world. It is the front line where the enemy uses other people, places and things to attack and destroy us. Remember Satan's goal, which is to kill or destroy all, especially the righteous!

That is the part of Spiritual Warfare that most people relate to when they first hear the subject. In later chapters I give a very through teaching on what is involved in arming oneself for this type of spiritual warfare. You will not have to be a victim any longer. You are about to receive the knowledge and tools to be an overcomer over all evil in your life.

In just a few weeks you will have the knowledge and spirit to be able to live each day free of the evil that is rising up in power during these last days,

You are starting a learning process that may change your life. It is truly one of the most exciting areas of our faith and it is so under taught. You are beginning the process of learning how to allow the spirit of God, the Holy Spirit within you, to rise up and overcome ALL EVIL. We serve such a wonderful and loving God. Through Him you can become one of the overcomers. Guaranteed!

If you do not have your textbook, entitled the "Biblical Spiritual Warfare Manual", you may visit our little Spiritual Warfare Store to get your copy. It is an ebook, not a printed book. The store transactions are handled by Paypal and the store is very tightly secured for your protection. It is also available at Amazon Kindle ebooks. This is an ebook. It downloads into your computer or pdf reader..

Go to- http://thejosephplan.org/book-store/product/biblical-spiritual-warfare-manual/

If you are part of a spiritual warfare and deliverance ministry, please contact the ministry and introduce yourself. We need to get to know one another. We can help you bring these teachings into your group at very little cost, if any.

God Bless!

Lesson Two

Understanding the problem

W E ARE INVOLVED **in a Spiritual battle of our lives. It is a battle where our enemy, the demonic, wants to ruin our relationship with God, ruin our testimony and make us sick or even worse, to kill us. He wants us living in sin, denying Jesus or dead.**

The promise of God is that if we are true believers and followers of His ways, He will protect us. In the Word He also gives us the tools to rise up and be overcomers. Yes we can develop the skills to take dominion over all evil.

As a Christian we are posed with a question. Can we determine if our problems are simply being caused by the fallen natural world? Or are we under demonic attack by the enemy? The answer is very important. It will broaden all of our understanding of the world in which we live.

But in order to do this we must have a basic understanding of who our enemy is.

As followers of Jesus Christ, what should our perspective be toward the spirit world? If we are willing to believe the Bible, we see that Satan is not only very real and very powerful, but God clearly commands us not to get involved with him or the occult (closely associated with Satan) in any way. Let's try to understand why.

Who are Satan and his demons?

The Bible reveals that Satan was originally created as "Lucifer," which means "light bringer." At some point he chose to rebel against his Creator (Isaiah 14:12-15).

Ezekiel wrote about him, saying, "You were perfect in your ways from the day you were created, till iniquity was found in you" (Ezekiel 28:15). There was no sin, no evil, no disharmony in all God had created. This changed with the rebellion of Lucifer.

When this first rebellion occurred, Lucifer, whose name was then changed to Satan, (which means "adversary"), recruited one third of the angels to rebel with him against God. It must have been a horrid rebellion. Lucifer wanted to be "as God" or "a God". They rebelled, were defeated and cast out of the third heaven down to earth. Satan and the rebelling angels, now known as demons, have been restrained here on earth since that time (Job 1:7; Revelation 12:3-4). Instead of being the "light bringer," Satan came to be known as a ruler of darkness (Ephesians 6:12). They fell from the dimension of light to the dimension of darkness.

Even though they were defeated by God in the third heaven, the demons have not given up their goal of trying to destroy whatever God creates in our dimension.

Can we understand the nature of demons and evil spirits? The following is referenced from www.biblestudy-tools.com.

Biblical references to Demons or Devils (demons are little devils)

Devils or demons? To the reality and personality of demons the N.T. scriptures have a lot to say. They were all created as angels, but are not to be confused with the angels now serving God and us, spoken of in *2 Peter 2:4* ; *Jude 1:6* .

Demons are spirits *Matthew 12:43 Matthew 12:45* are Satan's emissaries ; *Matthew 12:26 Matthew 12:27* ; *25:41* and so numerous as to make Satan's power practically ubiquitous. *Mark 5:9* . They are capable of entering and controlling both men and beasts *Mark 5:8 Mark 5:11-13* and earnestly seek embodiment, without which, apparently, they are powerless for evil. ; *Matthew 12:43 Matthew 12:44* ; *Mark 5:10-12* . Demon influence and demon possession are discriminated in the N. T. Instances of the latter are ; *Matthew 4:24* ; *Matthew 8:16 Matthew 8:28 Matthew 8:33* ; *9:32* ; *12:22* ; *Mark 1:32* ; *Mark 5:15 Mark 5:16 Mark 5:18* ; *Luke 8:35* ; *Acts 8:7* ; *16:16* . They are unclean, sullen, violent, and malicious ; *Matthew 8:28* ; *9:23* ; *10:1* ; *Matthew 12:43* ; *Mark 1:23* ; *5:3-5* ; *Mark 9:17 Mark 9:20* ; *Luke 6:18* ; *9:39* . They know Jesus Christ as Most High God, and recognize His supreme authority; *Matthew 8:31 Matthew 8:32* ; *Mark 1:24* ; *Acts 19:15* ; *James 2:19* . They know their eternal fate to be one of torment ; *Matthew 8:29* ; *Luke 8:31* . They inflict physical maladies; *Matthew 12:22* ; *17:15-18* ; *Luke 13:16* but mental disease is to be distinguished from the disorder of mind due to demonical control. Demon influence may manifest itself in religion asceticism and formalism *1 Timothy 4:1-3* degenerating into uncleanness *2 Peter 2:10-12* . The sign of demon influence in religion is departing from the faith, i.e. the body of revealed truth in Gospel contained in the Scriptures. *1 Timothy 4:1* . The demons maintain especially a conflict with believers who would be spiritual and target them. ; *Ephesians 6:12* ; *1 Timothy 4:1-3* . All unbelievers are open to demon oppression and possession *Ephesians 2:2* .

The believer's resources, prayer and bodily control Matthew 17:21 "the whole armor of God" *Ephesians 6:13-18* . Exorcism in the name of Jesus Christ *Acts 16:18* was practiced for demon possession. One of the awful features of the apocalyptic judgments in which this age will end is an eruption of demons out the abyss. *Revelation 9:1-11* .

Evil spirits or demons cannot forcibly take total control or possession of a person against his or her will, as some people fear. But that does not mean that our enemies in the demonic world cannot influence and affect us. One of our goals in this teaching is to gain the knowledge and understandings so we do not allow them to take advantage of us (2 Corinthians 2:11). Our goal is to allow God to teach us and raise us up to be Overcomers! Something "churchianity" should have been doing all along.

Always remember, the natural spirit centers in our mind. When a demonic spirit is influencing our mind and body it is said to be "oppressing us" We are under "oppression".

Demonic oppression is the work of evil spirits or demons that urge us to sin, to deny God's word, to feel spiritually dead, and to be in bondage to sinful things. This oppressive work is performed by demons, which are fallen angels, who resist God, and who sinned in their first estate (*Jude 6*). They war against God, against God's people, and against unbelievers. Their goal is to bring as many people as possible into rebellion against God and condemnation in hell.

The demonic is very opportunistic. They take advantage of any un-repented sin in our lives and ones shortcomings like un-Godly Fear, Guilt, Shame, Anger, Resentments or false Pride. Demonic oppression can be experienced in various ways:

•   **Physical ailments** such as sleeplessness, nightmares, strong anxiety, self-mutilation, addictions, and physical illness.

•   **Spiritual deadness** that includes apathy and anger towards God, interest in false religious systems.

•   **Emotional upheaval** such as regular outbursts of anger, high and low emotional levels, self-justification, fear, hopelessness, abnormal fixations, etc.

•   **Financial difficulties** such as constant and unusual financial pressures. Sometimes numerous things can go wrong, all very quickly, and cause us great financial strain and stress. (Anxiety)

• **Separation from God** giving us those times when we feel so lonely, distant and seemingly unable to realize our relationship with God.

We can, whether we mean to or not, invite demonic influence into our minds. When Israel came into the Promised Land, God warned them not to allow anyone to practice witchcraft, cast spells or try to talk with the dead (Deuteronomy 18:9-14). We are not to allow people who practice such things into our personnel lives.

The reason for this prohibition is that by involving ourselves in these practices, we open up our minds to the direct influence of the demon world. It is as if we opened a door of our minds and invited an evil spirit to come on in!

Put in terms of today's practices, this would include tarot cards, Ouija boards, palm reading, horoscopes and psychics. It would also include filling our minds with music, books and movies of the occult. There is an added danger if we also give up control of our minds through the abuse of alcohol and drugs. Our minds are precious instruments, and

God expects us to carefully monitor what we allow to come in.

But the idea of having or being given a special "power" is an incredibly appealing idea to our pride and vanity. Satan knows this and uses it to his advantage.

In Matthew 4 we read that he even tried to get Jesus Christ to fall for his perverted reasoning. After showing Him all the kingdoms of the earth and their wealth and power, Satan said, "And saith unto him, All these things will I give thee, if thou wilt fall down and worship me." (Matthew 4:9). But Jesus understood the price of such a decision-worship of Satan meant losing His position as Savior and member of the God family. What will be the cost for us if we fall for the lie and worship Satan? Do you?

How Satan deceives us

Some of what we have talked about may seem quite extreme. What if you aren't involved with any of these practices? What if you don't worship Satan? If you don't go to horror movies, use Ouija boards or read bad books-then you are safe, right? Perhaps the most powerful way in which Satan influences human beings is through his power to broadcast attitudes. He is described as the "prince of the power of the air" (Ephesians 2:2). This seems to be a reference to his ability to transmit attitudes and tempting thoughts, and from this no one is immune.

Have you ever found yourself thinking an evil thought and wondered where it came from? Have you heard the comment "The devil made me do it"? The devil cannot make you do anything. But he can make something sound or feel so appealing that you are willing to choose to do it "on your own." Maybe the quote should be, "The devil tempted me to do it, and I gave in."

In Ephesians 6:12 we are told: "For we wrestle not against flesh and blood, but against principalities, against powers, against the rulers of the darkness of this world, against spiritual wickedness in high [places]."

We struggle with ourselves, with the unrighteous influences of our society and with the powerful attitudes and temptations presented to us by Satan and his demons. Temptation worked effectively against Adam and Eve, and it can work just as effectively against you and me!

How to resist demonic influence and be an Overcomer over all evil.

The answer is gaining the knowledge provided for us in the Word of God and living our lives under and IN the Authority of Jesus Christ! Our job is to find out how.

When we are under the authority of our Lord Jesus Christ, we have "the authority" to say:

"Under the authority of Jesus Christ and through the power of the Holy Ghost, I command _____ to come out of _____!" and "I rebuke you in the name of Yeshua, the Lord Jesus Christ"!

When proclaimed, all spirits must obey: All little demons, big demons, familiar spirits or unfamiliar spirits. They all must obey under the authority of Jesus Christ. But it is important that we are prepared for the battles that come upon us. It isn't just that simple.

How can we? By learning to be in submission to Him and His ways.

Living and operating under the authority of Jesus Christ, through the power of the Holy Spirit should be a goal of every true Christian. It is the ultimate of An Enduring Faith.

You are of God, little children, and you have overcome them, because He who is in you is greater than he who is in the world. 1John 4:4

Who is Jesus talking to here? He is talking to His children, all those who are saved and assured their salvation through Him. He is talking to His children who now have the Holy Spirit within them, we who have repented and made a decision to turn our will and our lives over to Him. He is talking to those Christians who have been born again.

Are you sure of your salvation? There is misinformation and non- biblical teachings in too many churches today. We have to know- that we know- that we are assured salvation through Christ.

How does one know for sure? How can one tell they have the Holy Spirit within them?

We will know-that we know Jesus Christ and are born again:

- When we- keep His commandments (1 John 2:3)

- When we- are in Christ by keeping His word (1 John 2:5)

- When- the love of God has truly been perfected in us by keeping Christ's word (1 John 2:5

- When at- the last hour, because antichrist is coming and many antichrists have appeared. (1 John 2:18)

- When-everyone who hates his brother is a murderer - you know that no murderer has eternal life (1 John 3:15)

• When-He who knows God listens to the [Scriptures], he who is not from God will not, By this we know the spirit of truth and the spirit of error. (1 John 4:6)

• When-We know we abide in God because He gave us His Holy Spirit (1 John 4:13)

• When-We are assured that we have eternal life (1 John 5:13)

Do you know Jesus?

When we are assured of our salvation--We just know! We aren't necessarily perfect, but we know perfectly, that we are one of His kids.

Are you saved from damnation, the eternal fate of many? Are you sure? Ask Him in prayer. Find out and be assured.

My friend, Are you confident where you are going to spend eternity when this all ends? There is an end for all of us, even maybe today.

The Spirit itself beareth witness with our spirit, that we are the children of God: Rom 8:16

There is only one way to know and be assured- Ask our Father in heaven in Jesus Christ's' name in prayer today.

One cannot assume or acquire the "Authority of the spirit of Jesus Christ" without absolute assurance of eternal salvation, through personal repentance and the gift of the sacrifice and the shedding of the Blood of Jesus Christ and the receiving of the "Holy Spirit". One must be Spirit Filled!

When we ask the Lord, in Jesus Christ's name, He assures us with His peace and understanding. If for any reason you question your salvation, go to a quiet place, alone, and talk to Jesus. Repent of your sins and commit your life to Him. Then go to a bible believing church and get baptized.

He is faithful! He always listens and always responds to our needs.

When we petition the Lord, in Jesus Christ's name, He assures us with His peace and understanding and freely hands out His gifts of the Spirit. You will find the Salvation Prayer and its accompanying teachings in the "Biblical Spiritual Warfare Manual".

Let's define the terms we will be using and relative questions.

Do all born again Christians have authority over the natural and spirit world? Yes, but so many of us have not been taught how to use it.

When a person is saved, filled with the Holy Spirit and baptized, do we automatically receive this authority?

Yes. But it usually needs to be activated. We can ask for an anointing from God that activates the gifts we have been given. This is often done by the placing on of hands and the prayers of another anointed Christian believer or pastor. The bible refers to it as "the stirring of the spirit" and the anointing, an important act that is often missed.

Authority-taken from Dictionary.com

authority -

The power to determine, adjudicate, or otherwise settle issues or disputes; jurisdiction; the right to control, command, or determine.

1. The power to determine, adjudicate, or otherwise settle issues or disputes; jurisdiction; the right to control, command, or determine

2.   A power or right delegated or given; authorization: Who has the authority to grant permission.

3.   A person or body of persons in whom authority is vested, as a governmental agency.

Synonyms for authority.

1. Rule, power, sway. Authority, control, influence, denotes a power or right to direct the actions or thoughts of others. Authority is a power or right, usually because of rank or office, to issue commands and to punish for violations: to have authority over subordinates. Control is either power or influence applied to the complete and successful direction or manipulation of persons or things: to be in control of a project. Influence is a personal and unofficial power derived from deference of others to one's character, ability, or station; it may be exerted unconsciously or may operate through persuasion: to have influence over one's friends. 3. Sovereign, arbiter.

What does it mean to be under the authority of Jesus Christ?

The following are some of the authorities or powers that are given to those who are born again, Holy Spirit filled members of the family and Kingdom of God, along with bible references. The following gifts are available to all baptized and filled with the Holy Spirit believers in Jesus Christ.

The following are some of the authorities or powers that are given to those who are born again, saved Christians.

• Authority to communicate with the Father (Heb.4:14-16; 10:19-21)

• Authority to communicate with Jesus Christ (Rom.8:33-34; Heb.7:25; 1.John.2:25-26)

• Authority to request things of the Father (John.15:16; 16:23-26)

• Authority over evil spirits (Mark.16:17; Acts 16:16-18)

• Authority over the physical universe (Matt.21:18-21; Luke.9:54)

• Authority to heal (Mark.16:18; Acts 3:1-6; 5:15)

• Authority to govern the church (Acts 15:1-32; 1 Cor.1:10; 5:1-7; 2Thess.3:6)

• Authority to proclaim the gospel (Matt.28:19-20; Mark.16:15; Acts 1:8)

• Authority over life and death (Acts 5:1-15; 1 Cor.5:3-5; Rev.11:3-5)

• Authority to resurrect the dead (Acts 9:36-42; 20:6-10)

• Authority to bring a curse on the wicked (Acts 13:8-11)

• Authority to baptize into the Family of God (Matt.28:19-20)

The above list is very impressive. Under the authority of Jesus Christ, many of our human problems can be dealt with. I urge you to take the time and understand each biblical lesson.

There are certain authorities and powers that are only given to the spiritual leaders of the elect. There are many gifts and authorities of spiritual powers given to the entire body of Christ. The Lord hands out powers and authorities as He determines.

Not everyone receives all of the attributes of the authorities or powers (1Cor.12:1-12), but each of the elect of God is given what they need, by the Holy Spirit, in order to successfully fulfill God's purpose for them. See Matt 7:7-11; 1.Cor 12:8-10; 13:1-13; James 1:5; 2Peter.1:5-8; 1John.5:14.

Many of us have been gifted authorities and powers that we do not realize we have and are not using. What a terrible shame. If a person has a specialized gift, such as those of a prophet, evangelist, or the discernment of spirits, that person is expected by God to use these gifts or authorities as God intended.

The scriptures do not reveal exactly how each person is made aware of the spiritual gifts they have been given. But those who have been given these special powers should know that they have them. How? By revelation from God.

Moses was told by God himself (Ex.3:15-22; 4:1-9); Elisha the prophet was told by Elijah the prophet; Christ told his disciples (Mk.3:14-15; Matt.28:19-20);

"And these signs shall follow them that believe; in my name they shall cast out devils . . . they shall lay hands upon the sick and they shall recover" (Mk.16:17-18 KJV).

In the book of Acts, we see that Peter used the power and authority that he had been given over the natural laws of this world, to heal a man who had been lame from birth:

"Now Peter and John went up together into the temple at the hour of prayer, being the ninth hour. And a certain man lame from his mother's womb was carried, whom they laid daily at the gate of the temple which is called Beautiful, to ask alms of them that entered into the temple; . . . then Peter, fastening his eyes upon him with John, said, Look on us. And he gave heed to them, expecting to receive something from them. Then Peter said, Silver and gold I have none; but such as I have I give you: In the name of Jesus

Christ of Nazareth rise and walk" (Acts 3:1-6 KJV). See also Acts 3:16.

Peter used the following words. The exact words are very important.

"Such as I have, I give you". This statement makes it very clear that Peter had the authority and power to heal the sick. When Peter said

"In the name of Jesus Christ of Nazareth rise and walk",

He was not only announcing by whose authority he was healing the man, but, he was also commanding the healing by the authority and power of Jesus Christ.

On his own Peter was powerless.

Acts 16:18 And this did she many days. But Paul, being grieved, turned and said to the spirit, I command thee in the name of Jesus Christ to come out the same hour.

When we are under the authority of our Lord Jesus Christ, we already have "the authority" to say:

"Under the authority of Jesus Christ and through the power of the Holy Ghost, I command _____ to come out of _____!"

When proclaimed, all spirits must obey: All little demons, big demons, familiar spirits or unfamiliar spirits. They all must obey under the authority of Jesus Christ.

One cannot replace parts of the above command with your own thinking. We are developing a discipline that is exact and we can call on in a moment's notice. When we are put in a dangerous situation or a position of need to take charge and "command the spirit world to correct action", these exact words must be the first thing we think of.

Over one third of the bible deals with this subject and yet many pastors insist that it is not relevant for today. But they are absolutely pertinent for this world right now.

Read the above command as many times as you need to memorize it. It will become your most important spiritual warfare tool. The most powerful spiritually commanding words you will be uttering

In order to speak to the spirit world under His authority, we have much more to learn.

Positional Authority

In order for spiritual warfare to be effective, the believer must be in a position of surrender or submission to God and His ways. The believer's heart should be in a state of repentance and a thorough examination of oneself should have been done before you attempt to use it. The spiritual health checklist request form, located at the bottom of this page, should actually be the first thing one does before conducting spiritual warfare. Every Christian needs to get their own house in order, before we have true Positional Authority. I strongly advise you to fill out the download request form, located in the addendum of the Biblical Spiritual Warfare Manual and get your free copy of the "Rapture ForeWarning Advisory" today. Use it to determine if your own house is in order. I encourage you to not skip this part. A healthy relationship with the Lord is the solid ground upon which we stand when conducting spiritual warfare. It is about fifteen pages and will help all to make absolutely sure you haven't adopted any of society's carnal teachings in to your life.

In the hands of a true believer, with a repentant and surrendered heart, one can truly see the mountains are moved. The enemy moved back. Victory over evil claimed.

Putting the Authority into action.

It is important for all of us to understand that operating IN or under the authority of Jesus Christ carries with it a responsibility. It is never to be used for our own devises or purposes. It is only to be utilized for promoting the kingdom of God or helping a member of the body of Christ. The only exception, and it really isn't an exception, is when the Holy Spirit puts it on your heart to heal or spiritually help someone, including yourself, for health, safety and wellbeing. Many souls have been won because of signs, wonders and Godly miracles. It is never to be done for our own glory or self-edification, or out of our natural spirit.

Allow me to summarize. The words you use are very important. The demonic is usually not going to pay much attention to you if you are operating on your own authority. When we are In God's authority the bible tells us what we should say. Any deviation from these commands can not only hurt your chances for success, but it could cause a situation that actually empowers or just gets the spirit you are confronting all worked up.

Romans 13:1-7 "All scripture is given by the inspiration of God, and is profitable for doctrine, for reproof, for correction, and for instruction in righteousness so that the man of God may be perfect, thoroughly furnished to all good works" (2.Tim.3:16-17 KJV).

John.14:12-14 KJV "Truly, truly, I say to you, He that believes on me, the works that I do shall he do also; and greater works than these shall he do; because I go to the Father.

And whatsoever you shall ask in my name, that I will do, that the Father may be glorified in the Son. If you shall ask any thing in my name, I will do it".

Mark.16:17-18 KJV "And these signs shall follow them that believe; In my name they shall cast out devils; they shall speak with new languages; They shall take up serpents; and if they shall drink any deadly thing, it shall not hurt them; ......they shall lay hands on the sick, and they shall recover". See also Acts 1:4-5, 8; 5:1-15; 6:8; 13:8-11; 15:12.

If you consider yourself to be under demonic attack, I encourage you to study this teaching carefully. Spiritual warfare works best when it is conducted in a small group setting or with a prayer warrior partner. However there is much you can do when you are alone or in prayer. The following lesson is your manual and reference guide. Read it slowly and pray about what the Lord is teaching you. Do not try to grasp all of this overnight. Much of this is very deep learning's.

Study and pray about what is contained here. The Holy Spirit will guide you.

RULE # 1 NEVER challenge the devil himself. Satan. Lucifer. That is God's job and God's alone. Do not ever attempt to "BIND" him. That is left up to God.

RULE #2 Before you practice serious spiritual warfare you should examine yourself and make sure you are not deceiving yourself by living with or in any of the works of the flesh or sin. We have a special 15 page report entitled: the Rapture ForeWarning Advisory in the Addendum of this Manual.

RULE #3 Are you saved? Only you can know for sure. If you are a truly saved, born again, Holy Spirit filled Christian you already have the spiritual authority to precede with this teaching. If you are not sure you are saved, please stop right here and get the job done. This is a serious activity that should not be delved into alone by an unsaved or immature Christian. Yes, there are differences.

Living under the Authority of Jesus Christ requires one to believe that the Spirit within them (the Holy Spirit) is truly more powerful and does indeed give you a new strength that you didn't have before. In the next study we will be delving into how we can grow in our belief and increase our Faith. Thus our Spiritual Authority.

It is not by our power or authority. It is all, only because of Jesus, Jesus Christ!

Now please study "How to Overcome all, with your God Given Strength" in the Manual.

Please read chapter three before the next Spiritual Warfare Lesson. Together we can grow, overcome and be of service to God, the body of Christ and ourselves.

Spiritual Warfare Training special note-

Congratulations on making the decision to take the Spiritual Warfare Training series from The Joseph Plan. People from all over the world are starting this study program every day. They are taking it for varying reasons. It doesn't matter what your motivation is for participating, the important thing is that you are.

Allow me to introduce myself. My name is Thomas Holm, an ordained, non-denominational minister of the Gospel of Jesus Christ. I have almost six years of post-graduate training. (The "Christian" denomination) I left that denomination for doctrine reasons over ten years ago to become a non-denominational evangelist and care pastor. As or even more important is that God gave me this ministry by revelation through a vision. I reflect on this and two other visions onsite at The Joseph Plan. It is my hope and prayer that you are finding your experience here rewarding.

Spiritual Warfare can be a hard topic for many of us. It is not taught in most churches and there are many flavors offered out in the world. What you will learn here is Biblical Spiritual Warfare. No hocus-pocus. No physiological games, just teachings that come straight from the Word of God and out of the experience of some of the greatest men of God that live today.

What you have started and are about to learn is taken from the Word of God. The Holy Bible. It is the one book that we can put our faith in as being true and dependable. It is also the one book that gives us the teachings that will empower us to become true overcomers of the evil that is rising today and true spiritual warriors.

Studying the bible can get some of us all riled up. It should. It is called the Word of God for a reason. Its truths sometimes hurt. The reasoning's of man are always temporary and fleeting. The Word is eternal and spoken to us as the final authority. God's Word always trumps the words of man and it isn't spoken to make each one of us "feel good". It was given to us to save our souls and to provide us with a way of living that is indeed the softer and gentler way.

The Word of God also provides us with the spiritual truths that take dominion over the entire spiritual world. If you are new or uncomfortable with bible studies, I strongly suggest that you examine yourself. Find out why. Then say a prayer for the Lord to help you receive the truth, according to His Word that will help you to be an overcomer in these last days.

. Please believe me when I tell you that the entire world, including you, is in the spiritual battle of the ages and the demonic is rising everywhere. You do not have to be a victim of the chaos and destruction that is coming upon the world.

You will need the course textbook to satisfactorily finish this course. It is in our little book store at *http://www.thejosephplan.org/book-store/* and in Amazon Kindle books. There are no tests on completion. Your test will be a test of your spirit. If you do the suggested work your spirit will be flying.

The textbook is the "Biblical Spiritual Warfare Manual" by Rev or Pastor Thomas Holm. Together we can overcome evil and walk free IN Christ, our strength and protector.

Lesson Three

Obtaining the Authority over the enemy

Obtaining the Authority to overcome all Evil!

MY FRIEND, God through Jesus Christ, can overcome any and all of the evil in your life. Do you believe that? In this study we are dealing with and trying to understand some very deep spiritual concepts. We reference the bible and teach specific bible verses. We do that because they are very important to grasp and eventually learn. You don't have to understand everything the first time through. Keep these teachings in a file and use them as an additional reference guide to The Biblical Spiritual Warfare Manual. Together they may save your life some day. After this lesson things are going to loosen up somewhat as start talking about prayers and application.

In this lesson we are going examine the nature of God and how we can develop the type of relationship with Him that will empower us, through His Spirit, to overcome all evil

Are you taking this seriously and getting yourself prepared to fight the good fight?

If you are, when all this comes to an end, we who have been guaranteed salvation, thus born again, will be able to look back and be well satisfied, especially if we answer God's call on our lives.

We will then understand and praise Him even more! Always remember that in the last chapter of the Bible, GOD, you and I win!! If you make the decision to include yourself! Especially if you raise your hand and offer to be included as one member of the body of Christ that He can depend on for the days ahead. There is a war going on and it is coming to your town too, if it already hasn't. A spiritual war like this world has never seen.

Under normal times we Christians were always expected to be strong and to be bold in our faith. We have always been under spiritual attack because of our beliefs and the changing norms of society. But it is getting different now and the battle lines are getting easier to define and the enemy is getting empowered and bolder.

We have all been taught that we must have faith to succeed as a Christian. Faith is one of the primary tenets of our Christian religion. In this lesson we are taking a look at:

"How can we develop the type of faith that will cause the evil one and all his demons to flee from us"?

In order to develop the type of faith that we will need, we are going to have to believe. Believe that God IS and that only He has the power and authority to overcome all that we are exposed too in these final days. We need to establish our faith on THE ROCK!

The Rock of Strength, Power and Authority. Jesus Christ!

Phi 4:13 I can do all things through Christ which strengtheneth me.

The wise man built his house (faith) upon the Rock-Jesus Christ through His Word!

Yes, we need to believe that only He, Jesus Christ, Yeshua, has the power and authority to make all of creation tremble at His command.

Here is a wonderful short video teaching on God's strength that I recommend you watch.

http://thejosephplan.org/strength-a-bible-study/

The level of strength needed for maximum spiritual warfare seems to be proportionate to the type of faith we all will need to walk through all the trials and tribulations of the coming months and years. NOT being a victim.

I suggest we all read Psalm 91 daily for as long as the full meaning takes to fully enter our soul. God IS our Protector. God IS our Defender and God IS our Strength!

Psalm 91 is a base teaching that we can all start to build the foundation of our house upon.

http://thejosephplan.org/psalm-91-with-commentary-a-foundational-teaching-of-the-joseph-plan/

The big lesson of Psalms 91 is "who" is going to keep us safe and do the battle until the end. This applies to believers who are born again Christians. Are you confident where you are going to spend eternity when all this ends? There is an end for all of us some day, for some of us, it maybe today.

Each and every one of us, including you, need to ask very seriously. Do you know absolutely that you are a son or daughter of God? Do you know that you are assured eternal salvation?

Are You Saved from damnation, the eternal fate of so many? Are you sure? Because if you are, God provides you with all the tools you will need to live a life that is free of demonic oppression.

There is only one way to know. Ask The Father. Ask Him in prayer and find out. Be assured.

There is only one way to know and be assured- Ask our Father in heaven, in Jesus Christ's name, in prayer today!

Rom 8:16 The Spirit Himself bears witness with our spirit that we are the children of God and saved.

The following was taken from two chapters in my second spiritual warfare book, "Break the Bondage of Fear". It explains the subject matter very well.

When we ask the Lord, in Jesus Christ's name, He assures us with His peace and understanding. If for any reason you question your salvation, go to a quiet place, alone, and talk to Jesus. Repent of your sins and commit your life to Him. Then go to a bible believing church and get baptized.

He is faithful! He always listens and always responds!

Yes, He is very, very faithful and you are not THE Exception!

We go to a quiet place and humble ourselves before the one true living and eternal God.

(That most likely means kneeling down before Him)

But don't worry about where He is. Our God is Omnipresent. Which means He is available everywhere and will deal with you where-ever you go to.

We submit to Him in prayer. We repent of our sins and sinful thoughts and turn our will and lives over to His care. We surrender to Him and all His ways.

"For whosoever shall call upon the name of the Lord shall be saved." Romans 10:13

"For all have sinned and come short of the glory of God" Rom 3:23

"For the wages of sin is death, but the gift of God is eternal life through Jesus Christ our Lord." Romans 6:23

"Because if you confess the Lord Jesus, and believe in your heart that God has raised Him from the dead, you shall be saved." Romans 10:9.

"For with the heart one believes unto righteousness, and with the mouth one confesses unto salvation." Romans 10:10

It's all between you and God. This may be your moment. Please don't let it pass. God's tugging at your heart right now!

If you want to be assured eternal salvation today, just pray this simple prayer with sincerity, humility and from the bottom of your soul. Print it out and read it, if you need to. But mean it! Pray it from your heart. If you have never done this I beg you too.

Is it time to stop everything and make sure of your eternal salvation and thus your relationship with God? If it is, I invite you, right now to go to a quiet place and pray the following prayer. (Download any corporate church teachings that are getting in your way). This may be your big opportunity. You will be joining His family and taking a big step in receiving the power from God to Overcome your fears and a whole lot more.

"Dear Jesus, I believe in You. I believe You are the only Son of God and that You shed your blood and died for my sins, and that you were buried and rose again as it is written in the bible. I declare that you are 100% God. I'm sorry for the things I've done, the sins I have committed. Forgive me for all my sins Lord Jesus.

Come into my heart today Lord Jesus, take charge of my life and make me the way You want me to be. With Your ever present help, I renounce all my sinful practices of the past. Cleanse my heart with Your precious blood. I believe You are the creator and the only way to salvation. I surrender my will and my life to you. Please fill me with your Holy Spirit. In Jesus Christ's holy name I ask, Amen"

My friend, if you prayed that prayer and meant it from the bottom of your heart, your eternal salvation is assured! You will never be alone again! Please make sure that you get baptized soon and ask to receive the Holy Spirit. You are becoming part of something that is so special and that will be with you for the rest of your days. Your eternal destiny has just been assured. No amount of "good works" could do what you are doing today! And this eternal gift is free! You can now live each and every day with *An Enduring Faith* that will help you to overcome all obstacles and all your fears.

You now are assured that you have joined His family and that He is now in charge of your security. Psalm 91 can now come alive for you.

You may have said that prayer for the first time or maybe to reaffirm your commitment to the Lord. If you did, for whatever reason-- Congratulations.

If you did say that prayer I advise you to take some time right now and meditate on your new relationship with our Heavenly Father and the Son, Yeshua, Jesus Christ. You should go as soon as possible to a bible believing church or anointed Christian and get baptized to receive the Holy Ghost or Spirit.

Do you believe that God can and will, if you ask?

Do you believe that God, through Jesus Christ, can and will Overcome all evil and keep you safe.

An Enduring Faith is a faith in God, Our Lord Jesus Christ, that will carry and sustain us through the trying and dangerous times that we live in.

An Enduring Faith is a faith in God that will Overcome all the obstacles of these coming days. Victoriously!

Living with An Enduring Faith can only happen if our Eternal Salvation is assured!

An Enduring Faith is not a suggested replacement to your churches doctrine of faith as long as that doctrine is biblically based.

At the Heart of An Enduring Faith is the Gospel of Jesus Christ. As stated in the New Testament of the Holy Bible.

He or she that walks and lives with an Enduring Faith will be kept Safe from the evil one during these evil days! This is one of the great promises of God in Matthew 24. Jesus returning to gather His children and bring them home, to spare them of His wrath to come is a great promise during times of trouble.

Mat 24:13 But he who endures to the end, the same shall be kept safe.

Matthew 24 tells us to endure to the end. End of what? End of time? End of the age? End of the tribulation?

Rom 8:38 For I am persuaded, that neither death, nor life, nor angels, nor principalities, nor powers, nor things present, nor things to come,

Rom 8:39 Nor height, nor depth, nor any other creature, shall be able to separate us from the love of God, which is in Christ Jesus our Lord.

He or she that walks and lives with an Enduring Faith, to the end of our time, will be kept Safe from temptation, the Evil One and all his minions! We are the generation that will meet the Lord "In the Clouds".

The answer to our daily problems is to walk with a faith and belief that the Lord has accomplished everything. A faith that assures you that your sins have been forgiven. A faith that will strengthen, protect and carry you through all evil for all your days! A faith that has set you free!

Always try and remember, the spirit of fear or any other worker of Satan cannot exist in the presence of God.

The Scriptures speak the absolute truth. They are the Word of God. They can guide us in whatever situation we are in and through any trouble we find ourselves up against.

Take the time to search and meditate on the Word of God daily and find the answer to your problems and concerns. Overcome them.

"He has given us His very great and precious promises..." 2 Peter 1:4

These promises are put on our heart by Christ, if we are born again. They are taught in the Bible and confirmed by the Holy Spirit. The Lord wants us to realize these promises as truths every day.

The Word was given to us to teach us and encourage us.

"The Lord will keep you from all harm--he will watch over your life; the Lord will watch over your coming and going both now and forevermore." Psalm 121:7, 8

"When you pass through the waters, I will be with you; and when you pass through the rivers, they will not sweep over you. When you walk through the fire, you will not be burned; the flames will not set you ablaze." Isaiah 43:1, 2

"But whoever listens to me will live in safety and be at ease, without fear of harm" Proverbs 1:33.

WE MUST BELIEVE in the Gospel of Jesus Christ. Not the gospels that man promotes. We need to believe that Jesus can and will do for us what we cannot do for ourselves.

Believe on Jesus for life---Eternal Life---Mankind is trying, but will fail!

John 6:40 And this is the will of Him who sent Me, that everyone who sees the Son and believes on Him should have everlasting life. And I will raise him up at the last day.

John 6:41 Then the Jews murmured about Him, because He said, I am the bread which came down from Heaven.

John 6:42 And they said, Is this not Jesus the son of Joseph, whose father and mother we know? How now does this One say, I have come down from Heaven?

John 6:43 Jesus therefore answered and said to them, Do not murmur with one another.

John 6:44 No one can come to Me unless the Father who has sent Me draw him, and I will raise him up at the last day.

John 6:45 It is written in the Prophets, "And they shall all be taught of God." Therefore everyone who hears and learns from the Father comes to Me.

John 6:46 Not that anyone has seen the Father, except He who is from God, He has seen the Father.

John 6:47 Truly, truly, I say to you, He who believes on Me has everlasting life.

Let us repeat that again. Anyone, he or she, that truly believes on or in Jesus Christ will be saved and have eternal life! Wow! That was Jesus talking.

Rom 10:13 For everyone, "whoever shall call on the name of the Lord will be saved."

John 12:46 "I have come into the world as light, so that no one who believes in me should stay in darkness."

John 1:12 "Yet to all who received him, to those who believed in his name, He gave the right to become children of God."

AND we will receive a lot more.

Believe on Jesus and receive PEACE

John 14:27 "Peace I leave with you, my peace I give you. I do not give as the world gives. Do not let your hearts be troubled and do not be afraid."

Phil. 4:7 "And the peace of God, which transcends all understanding, will guard your hearts and your minds in Christ Jesus."

Believe on Jesus and receive True LOVE

Proverbs 8:17 "I love those who love me, and those who seek me find me."

Jeremiah 31:3 "I have loved you with an everlasting love; I have drawn you with loving-kindness."

1 Cor. 2:9 "No eye has seen, no ear has heard, no mind has conceived what God has prepared for those who love him."

Believe on Jesus and receive True JOY

John 15:11 "I have told you this so that my joy may be in you and your joy maybe complete"

Believe on Jesus and receive True JOY

John 15:11 "I have told you this so that my joy may be in you and your joy maybe complete"

Father, please help me and bring joy back into my life. I want so much to have a joyful and peaceful life.

In Jesus' name I ask.

Amen

John 16:22 "...but I will see you again and you will rejoice, and no one will take away your joy.

Believe on Jesus and receive PROTECTION AND STRENGTH.

Psalm 91 He who dwells in the secret place of the Most High shall rest under the shadow of the Almighty.

1 Chronicles 16:11 Seek the LORD and his strength; seek his presence continually!

Exodus 15:2 The LORD is my strength and my song, and he has become my salvation; this is my God, and I will praise him, my father's God, and I will exalt him.

Philippians 4:13 I can do all things through him who strengthens me.

Real Courage

Isaiah 40:29 "He gives strength to the weary and increases the power of the weak"

Isaiah 43:1 " Fear not, for I have redeemed you; I have summoned you by name; you are mine"

Believe on Jesus and receive True Faith

Heb.11:1 "Now faith is being sure of what we hope for and certain of what we do not see"

Gal. 3:26 "You are all sons of God through faith in Christ Jesus".

2 Cor. 5:7 "We live by faith, not by sight"

Believe on Jesus and receive Comfort

Psalm 46:1 "God is our refuge and strength, an ever present help in trouble."

John 16:33 "I have told you these things, so that in me you may have peace. In this world you will have trouble. But take heart! I have overcome the world! "

Matt. 11:28 "Come to me, all you who are weary and burdened, and I will give you rest."

Believe on Jesus and receive Mercy

Isaiah 30:18 "...the Lord longs to be gracious to you; he rises to show you compassion. For the Lord is a God of justice. Blessed are all who wait for him! "

Psalm 103:13 "As a father has compassion on his children, so the Lord has compassion on those who fear him."

Believe on Jesus and receive Guidance

Psalm 32:8 "I will instruct you and teach you in the way you should go; I will counsel you and watch over you."

Isaiah 42:16 "I will lead the blind by ways they have not known, along unfamiliar paths I will guide them, I will turn the darkness into light before them and make the rough places smooth. These are the things I will do; I will not forsake them."

Believe on Jesus and be LED BY THE HOLY SPIRIT AND HIS WORD - TO BE AT PEACE THROUGH ALL THINGS

Gal 5:24 But those belonging to Christ have crucified the flesh with its passions and lusts.

Gal 5:25 If we live in the Spirit, let us also walk in the Spirit.

Believe on Jesus and WALK WITH HIM - ALL POWER GIVEN TO HIM

Mat 28:18 And Jesus came and spoke unto them, saying, All power is given unto me in heaven and in earth.

Mat 28:19 Go ye therefore, and teach all nations, baptizing them in the name of the Father, and of the Son, and of the Holy Ghost:

Mat 28:20 Teaching them to observe all things whatsoever I have commanded you: and, lo, I am with you always, even unto the end of the world. Amen.

Walking with An Enduring Faith, He will never forsake US

Living one day at a time, in the confidence of an ENDURING FAITH that Jesus Christ CAN and WILL protect, sustain and guide us is our assurance to you.

The most import part of An Enduring Faith is that we have the right relationship with Him! Only then can we be at peace with and under the authority of our creator--Jesus Christ. Simply knowing about Jesus Christ is far from the entire answer. Simply attending church and trying to be a good person is not going to sustain and protect you.

I invite you to listen to a wonderful presentation of the Gospel of Jesus Christ by Pastor Erik Ludy. It is a You Tube video. If you cannot open it, copy and paste it into a browser. It will be well worth it. It is a beautiful presentation.

http://www.youtube.com/embed/nPlOkdNL-QQ

Do you believe that God can and will help you, if you ask and allow Him too? Do you believe that Jesus has the power and authority to take charge in your life over all evil?

The lesson so far is that if we can believe on Jesus Christ and trust In Him, He and only He has the power to Overcome all evil and fear, in and around our lives. I ask you. Do you believe? Have you put your faith and trust In Him?

Only He is strong enough to empower us to be a true overcomer over all evil in our lives. Do you believe?

In the next lesson we will be studying how you can develop the spiritual authority to be a Spiritual Warrior and an overcomer over all the world can through at us. Next week I am including a study that has been downloaded and read by thousands of people on The Joseph Plan. It deals with the "Works of the Flesh" The norms of societies that we can fall into believing it is OK. Not realizing the danger they are putting us into. We are in the final age and I encourage you to read and study the following carefully. It will possibly reveal to you the opening for the demonic you have created in your life. With these doors left open you will never be assured of a faith that WILL OVERCOME ALL EVIL.

God Bless and May the God of all of creation keep you safe!

End of Lesson Three

Lesson Four

Seek Righteousness, Gain Power

Examine oneself and seek righteousness and authority.

Eliminating the open doors one can have for the demonic.

SOME OF YOU WILL RECOGNIZE this lesson. Most of it has been available on The Joseph Plan and downloaded by thousands. It was originally written as a guide to help all of us to be prepared for the soon coming return of our Lord Jesus Christ. It is entitled the Rapture ForeWarning Advisory.

But it applies directly to our teaching series on spiritual warfare. The following is a study about the works of the flesh as mentioned in the book of Galatians chapter five.

Is there something in your life that can be providing an open door for the demonic and possibly disqualify you from Salvation and the Rapture? Is there something in your life that can be an invitation for the demonic to oppress and control your life? This is a spiritual warfare teaching and not a general introduction to Christian living. But these questions are all too often neglected when we discuss these important issues.

If you are a slave to any of the "Works of the Flesh"---you may be at risk of being separated from the spirit of God or blocked from finding Him in the first place.

This is your invitation to "Examine oneself".

This study focuses on the primary reasons why living our life according to society's standards can be an open door and an invitation for trouble with the demonic. As you study this Advisory please be honest with your own situation and life style.

Living with the "Works of the Flesh" is living in sin.

You, especially You, ARE NOT THE EXCEPTION.

"Works of the Flesh" Galatians 5:19-21

1 Thessalonians 5:21 Test (Examine) all things, and hold firmly that which is good.

Every Christian is told by the Lord to "Examine oneself"

A Study from The Joseph Plan *www.thejosephplan.org*

Can a Christian lose their salvation? If you are a saved, born again Christian, the answer is NO! God doesn't change His mind. He choose you from the beginning. When saved and infilled by the Holy Spirit, an obedient person cannot be a slave to any of the "Works of the Flesh". We can make bad choices because of the lack of knowledge and commit sin, but the Blood of Jesus will cover all, when we repent. But we must repent.

By the grace and power of God and the sacrifice of Jesus Christ you are assured an eternity in heaven. Because of your assurance of salvation you cannot be disqualified.

Please see the post entitled "Can a Christian lose their Salvation?" on The Joseph Plan website if you need any more reference.

The reason Jesus Christ had to be crucified and die on that cross was because He knew none of us could achieve salvation on our own merits. Only the power of the cross and the blood were enough to give us the grace we needed to receive forgiveness and salvation.

All of us came into this world with a fallen nature or spirit. If left to our own devices we would all be disqualified from salvation. That means you and me and everyone. We would all be living in the "Works of the Flesh" and a sinful lifestyle.

What are the "Works of the Flesh"?

The "Works of the Flesh" keep us from living righteous lives. Left to our own best thinking we all would be involved in the "Works of the Flesh". If man is not renewed and his natural spirit transformed, it is what the natural man will manifest or become by his own will power. He or she will develop one or more of these natural traits. It is common to all people and none of us are an exception. If any of these are allowed to flourish, one becomes in bondage to them and they can control ones thinking, emotions, actions and very life. They can become a stronghold from which the demonic is given legal permission to operate. It becomes the "base of operations" from which the demonic conducts its business. They are all sin. Any of the "Works of the Flesh" will establish a base of operations for the demonic to conduct its war against our soul.

The Works of the Flesh are the primary way the demonic is given permission to mess with us, influence our

thoughts and cause us pain and misery! Even cause great harm and death, which is its ultimate goal.

They can also cause a person to be:

"Disqualified from the Rapture" and "Oppressed by the Demonic".

This is an important issue. If you are truly saved, a true Christian, you are assured Salvation and a seat on the first flight out of here in the Rapture. You'll be swooped up into the clouds in the Rapture to meet Jesus and brought to the mercy seat. Praise the Lord! Free at last! One thing that the Joseph Plan teaches consistently is that the Bible does not tell us that we can lose our Salvation. It is eternal, and a gift to us from God. It does say that we can push the Holy Spirit away however. As Christians, we may lose our fellowship with Him, as a result of our selfish desires, but we can never lose His promise of our salvation (Hebrews 10:17). In Heb. 12:4-11, we see that God has disciplinary measures to His children who persist in sinning.

In Gal. 5:16-21, the Apostle Paul is admonishing the Christian to commit his life to the control (i.e. constantly) of the Holy Spirit, and to not surrender to the flesh. If one daily commits him or herself to the Holy Spirit's (God's) control, the law won't bother us, since He constantly and consistently is desirous of allowing the His Spirit to control and guide us. On the other hand, one who constantly lives in bondage to and after the flesh may not have the Holy Spirit in them and its regeneration of life. At the very least the Holy Spirit is greatly repressed and thus distant or pushed away. Thereby living a consistently self-centered, unrighteous life and will not inherit eternal life. I'm not saying that a Christian never partakes of sinful, self-centered actions I'm saying that if those things control one's life, then it is certain he was never saved to begin with, Or has made extremely bad decisions, thus separated from Christ and must come home to Him. Many good people are separated.

We are not to judge other people. Only God can be the judge of someone else's salvation and eternal destiny. But we are told to judge ourselves. This is self-examination.

How can we figure all this out? Simply by taking your own inventory.

So, all of us spending some time and taking an inventory is a good thing. The bible gives us a wonderful list that we can use to discover if we have fallen into the trap of living in sin.

The Word of God says in Galatians chapter five:

Gal 5:19 Now the works of the flesh are clearly revealed, which are: adultery, fornication, uncleanness, lustfulness,

Gal 5:20 idolatry, sorcery, hatreds, fightings, jealousies, angers, rivalries, divisions, heresies,

Gal 5:21 envying, murders, drunkennesses, revelings, and things like these; of which I tell you before, as I also said before, that they who do such things shall not inherit the kingdom of God.

Here are the definitions and meanings of each of character traits, habit or characteristics mentioned as Works of the Flesh. They are taken from Galatians in the Bible and the sources footnoted below. I encourage you to read the entire list and EXAMINE YOURSELF. Take an honest inventory of your life. If you find that one or more of these traits FITS, you will want to read on. This will not do you any good or be of benefit if you are not totally honest with yourself.

We are going to start with the definitions as taken from Strongs Biblical Concordance and the classical language definitions. Strong's is one of the most widely accepted bible references available. This is not a list of order of importance or any kind of ranking. The works are listed in the order they appear in the bible.

If you are wondering or looking for answers about yourself and your involvement with any of the "Works of the Flesh" that could be the entry point for your problems with evil and "Disqualify" you from salvation and thus the rapture, we are providing you with the following list of behaviors and there definitions. We are doing our best to help you know for sure and to leave one with "NO wiggle room". I encourage you to take this very seriously. Your spiritual fitness is what you are testing.

2Co 13:5 Test yourselves and find out if you really are true to your faith. If you pass the test, you will discover that Christ is living in you. But if Christ isn't living in you, you have failed.

Yes, Examine one's self. Test yourself in a very deep and prayerful examination.

1 Thessalonians 5:21 Test (Examine) all things, and hold firmly that which is good.

Now is the time to take an honest inventory. The Bible has all the answers for you.

This may be one of the most important issues you have faced in your entire life. Are you saved from eternal damnation? And, are you disqualified for the rapture? Are you providing the demonic an open door to oppress and influence you?

The references are provided below.

1. **Adultery-** Having sex with someone other than your spouse. (see Matt.15:19; Mark 7:21; John 8:3; Gal.5:19) from #3431 - AV - commit adultery - 1) to commit adultery; 1a) to be an adulterer; 1b) to commit adultery with, have unlawful intercourse with another's wife; 1c) of the wife: to suffer adultery, be debauched; 1d) A Hebrew idiom, the word is used of those who at a woman's solicitation are drawn away to idolatry, i.e. to the eating of things sacrificed to idols.

It is a commandment: Thou shall not commit adultery! Ex 30:14

Making the decision to willfully live in a situation or lifestyle where you are regularly breaking this commandment puts one in supreme jeopardy.

Also see: 1Cor 6:9. Heb 13:4, James 4:4, Mark 7:21, Pro 6:32, Rev 2:22.

2. **Fornication** - To have sex with anyone outside of marriage. To commit fornication; commit - 1) to prostitute one's body to the lust of another; 2) to give one's self to unlawful sexual intercourse; 2a) to commit fornication outside of marriage; 3) metaphors. To be given to idolatry, to worship idols; 3a) to permit one's self to be drawn away by another into idolatry - found in - I Cor.6:18; 10:8 (twice); Rev.2:14, 20; 17:2; 18:3, 9

What we are talking about here is sexual behaviors which are contrary to God's law.

It is wide spread and sometimes seems like "everybody is doing it. Well, everyone isn't doing it. True Christians don't.

See also: *1Co 5:9-10, 1Co 7:1-2; Rev 9:21*

Sexual immorality brings punishment. An obstacle for salvation.

Heb 13:4, Lev 20:10-21; Pr 2:16-19; Pr 22:14; Eze 16:38; Ro 1:24-27; Eph 5:5;

Col 3:5-6; 1Th 4:3-6; Jude 7; Rev 21:8; Rev 22:15

Sexual immorality has no place in the Christian life

See also: *1Th 4:3,7 Ac 15:20,29; Ac 21:25; Ro 13:13; 1Co 6:9-11,13-20; 1Co 10:8; Eph 5:3; Col 3:5; Heb 12:16.*

Is it time to make the right decision? Time is short!

Paul writes a great deal about the "Works of the Flesh". He obviously considers them very important and wants us to seriously meditate and seek God's truths.

3. **Uncleanness** - To be morally or spiritually impure. 1) uncleanness; 1b) in a moral sense: the impurity of lustful, luxurious, profligate living; 1b1) of impure motives.

In a moral sense: unclean in thought and life.

To not be cleansed of filth impurity, etc., 1a) to prune trees and vines from useless shoots, 1b) metaphors. from guilt, to expiate - found in - John 15:2; Heb.10:2

See also: Matt 23:27, Rom 6:19, 1 Thess 4:7, 2 Peter 2:1

4. **Lustfulness or Lewdness** - To be lustful; act of being lustful, to be desirous of someone physically. lasciviousness, wantonness, filthy - 1) unbridled lust, excess, licentiousness, lasciviousness, wantonness, outrageousness, shamelessness, insolence. Excessively desiring, in the flesh, another person.

An overpowering and compulsive desire or passion, especially of a sexual nature. Scripture condemns lust of all kinds, and urges believers to show self-control.

See also: *Pro 6:25-29; Mat 5:28 Ge 3:6; Job 31:1; James 1:13-15; 1Jn 2:16*

5.   **Idolatry** - To worship of physical object as a god; immoderate attachment or devotion to something. The worship of false gods, idolatry; 1a) of the formal sacrificial feats held in honor of false gods; 1b) of avarice, as a worship of Mammon; 2) in the plural, the vices springing from idolatry and peculiar to it - found in I Cor.10:14; Gal.5:20; Col.3:5; I Peter 4:3

To worship an image, likeness; 1a) i.e. whatever represents the form of an object, either real or imaginary; 1b) used of the shades of the departed, apparitions, spectres, phantoms of the mind, etc.; 2) the image of a heathen god; 3) a false god.

It can fall under one of the Ten Commandments. Thou shalt not have any other god's before me.

What do you have in your life that you hold to a higher esteem or consider more important that your relationship with God?

See also: 1 Cor 8:7, 1 Cor 10:19, Eph 5:5, Rev 21:8, Rev 22:15, 1 Cor 10:14,

6.   **Sorcery** - Also called Witchcraft! Having spiritual intercourse with the devil. Sorcery, witchcraft - 1) the use of or the administration of drugs, 2) poisoning, 3) sorcery, magical arts, often found in connection with idolatry and fostered by it, 4) metaph. the deceptions and seductions of idolatry - found in - Gal.5:20; Rev.9:21; 18:23.

From pharmakon (a drug, i.e. spell-giving potion) - AV - sorcerer - 1) one who prepares or uses magical remedies, 2) sorcerer - found in - Rev.21:8.

Pharmakeia: sorcery, magical arts, often found in connection with idolatry.

Examples of those who practiced sorcery in the bible.

Egyptian magicians: *Ex 7:11; Ex 8:18 Balaam: Nu 22:6; Nu 23:23*

2Ki 21:6 Manasseh, king of Judah; *Isa 47:9-13* the Babylonians; *Ac 8:9-11* Simon of Samaria; *Ac 13:6-8* Bar-Jesus of Cyprus; *Ac 19:19* people in Ephesus

Also see: strongly forbidden

See also *Dt 18:9-12 Lev 19:26,31; Jer 27:9-10; Eze 13:18,20*

God's judgment comes upon sorcerers and magicians

Lev 20:6; Mic 5:12; Ac 13:6-11; Rev 21:8

Gal 5 God made participation in occult practices punishable by death.

That is serious and would make any of us disqualified. But a true Christian couldn't possibly participate in any of this. For a true Christian simply couldn't make that willful decision.

7.   **Hatreds** - To have prejudiced hostility. Enmity, hatred - 1) enmity, 2) cause of enmity - found in - Luke 23:12; Rom. 8:7; Gal. 5:20; Eph.2:15, 16; James 4:4

Hateful - enemy, foe - 1) hated, odious, hateful; 2) hostile, hating, and opposing another; 2a) used of men as at enmity with God by their sin; 2a1) opposing (God) in the mind; 2a2) a man that is hostile; 2a3) a certain enemy; 2a4) the hostile one; 2a5) the devil who is the most bitter enemy of the divine government. Hatred for others or God is associated with human sin. Scripture also emphasizes God's hatred of sin and evil. Believers are commanded to love those who hate them.

Hatred as evidence of corrupt human nature

See also: *2Sa 13:15; Tit 3:3 Ge 37:4; Dt 7:15; Dt 19:11-12; Jdg 11:7; 2Sa 13:22;*

Ps 25:19; Ps 38:19; Mt 24:10; Gal 5:19-20; 1Jn 2:9-11; 1Jn 3:15; 1Jn 4:20

Hatred of God himself

Ps 81:15; Ro 1:29-31 See also *Ex 20:5; Dt 7:10; Dt 32:41; 2Ch 19:2; Ps 50:17*

Jn 3:20; Jn 15:23-25; Jas 4:4

Hatred of Jesus Christ

See also: *Jn 7:7 Isa 53:3; Mt 12:14; Mt 21:46; Mt 26:3-4; Mt 27:22; Lk 19:14;*

Believers are to love those who hate them

See also: *Luke 6:27-28, Mt 5:43-44.*

8. **Contentions and Fighting** - A quarreler, continual debater, strife; to argue about most things. contention, contentious 1) electioneering or intriguing for office; 1a) apparently, in the NT a courting distinction, a desire to put one's self forward, a partisan and fractious spirit which does not disdain low arts; 1b) partisanship, fractiousness - Further note - This word is found before NT times only in Aristotle where it denotes a self-seeking pursuit of political office by unfair means. Paul exhorts us to be like Christ, not putting self forward or being selfish (Phil. 2:3). James 3:14 speaks against having selfishness or self-promoting in your heart.

Rom.2:8; II Cor.12:20; Gal.5:20; Phil.1:16; 2:3; James 3:14, 16

To stir up, excite, stimulate, to provoke - II Cor.2:9; Col.3:21

God hates violence

See: *Ps 11:5; Ps 139:19; Jer 22:3; Eze 45:9; Mal 2:16*, Prov 18:18, Jer 15:10,

Titus 3:9, James 4:1-2.

9.   **Jealousies** - Emulations, ambitious or envious rivalry. Embittered about another person's wealth, possessions or status. It is an emotion and typically refers to the   negative **thoughts** and **feelings** of insecurity, fear, and anxiety over an anticipated loss of something that the person values, particularly in reference to a human connection.

Jealousy often consists of a combination of presenting emotions such as **anger, resentment**, inadequacy, helplessness and **disgust**. It is not to be confused with **envy**.

Human jealousy arises from sin

Mk 7:21-23 Mt 15:19-20

Human jealousy can be destructive

Pr 14:30 Job 5:2; Pr 27:4; Ecc 9:5-6

Also see: *Gal 5:19-21, Ps 37:1-2; Pr 23:17; Ro 13:13; 1Co 13:4-7;*

Tit 3:3-5; Jas 3:14-16

10.   **Angers** - Violent anger; to pay back with punishment for an offense or crime. Anger or wrath. Wrath, fierceness, indignation - 1) passion, angry, heat, anger, forthwith boiling up and soon subsiding again. A strong emotion; a feeling that is oriented toward some real or supposed grievance.

In the temple Jesus had righteous anger in His actions and words in emptying the Temple precincts of the hucksters. (*Mark 11:15-17*).

There is righteous anger and unrighteous anger. This is talking about unrighteous self centered anger. Christians should be slow to anger, to make sure it isn't their lower self that isn't rising up. (James 1:19-20)

Anger can lead to Wrath.

Any unrighteous wrath by man is strictly forbidden. God will be pouring out His wrath upon the unrighteous after the Rapture of His church.

Gen 49:7, Isa 16:6, Lev 10:6, Deut 9:7, Nah 1:6,

We are commanded to love our neighbor. Love and wrath are opposites.

God holds the objects of His Wrath, the people, responsible for their actions.

Num 11:1; Deut 1:26-36; 13:2, 6, 13 et al.; Josh 7:1; 1 Sam 28:18;

Ps 2:1-6; 78:21, 22, Mark 9:43-48, Luke 12:5, Matt 7:13-27,

God's wrath is the punishment of the soul. *Matt 5:21, 22; 10:28*

11. **Strife** - Rivalries or selfish ambitions. Contentious quarrels; fond of strife. Lack of agreement or harmony. A bitter conflict; heated, often violent dissension.

Strife is usually caused by selfish ambitions. Selfishness causing untold amounts of pain and suffering. Some seen, much un-seen

Selfish Ambition is the pursuit of personal status and fortune, which is contrary to the purposes of God as expressed in Scripture.

See: *Pr 6:18; Eph 2:3; 1Jn 2:16*, Phil 2:3

12. **Divisions or dissensions** - Resistant to authority. Disagreements arising from diversity of opinions and goals. The act of separating into parts, causing people to loose

consensus, partitioning; basic mathematical operation in which one number is divided by another; department, faculty; group of soldiers that form a distinct tactical unit within a squadron.

13.   **Heresies** - An opinion or doctrine contrary to the biblical truth; It carries the connotation of behaviors or beliefs likely to undermine accepted morality and cause tangible evils, damnation, or other punishment. In some religions, it also implies that the heretic is in alliance with the religion's symbol of evil, such as Satan or chaos.

Within the church. *1 Cor. 11:19,*

In *Titus 3:10* a "heretical person" is one who is always challenging the truth and trying to lead in a contrary direction and should be avoided.

Heresies signify self-serving doctrines that do not emanate from God.

See: (*2 Pet. 2:1*).

1

4.   **Envy** - Resentment of an advantage enjoyed by another, joined with a desire to possess the same advantage. Envy is a sin of jealousy over the blessings and achievements of others.

Envy is a great desire to have something possessed by another.

Envy is the result of human sin

See: *Pr 23:17; Mt 15:19-20 Mk 7:21-23; Ro 1:29; 1Co 3:3; 1Ti 6:4;*

Tit 3:3; 1Pe 2:1-2

Love does not envy others

See: *1Co 13:4*

Of envy

Results See: *Job 5:2 Pr 14:30; Ecc 4:4; Jas 3:14-16*

Envy forbidden

See: *Ps 37:1 Pr 3:31; Pr 24:1; Gal 5:26*

15. **Murders -** Murder is the unlawful killing, with malice and aforethought of another human, and generally this state of mind distinguishes murder from other forms of homicide (such as manslaughter).

To Murder is strictly against the Ten Commandments.

Thou shalt not kill.

Kill in the original language means "to murder."

16. **Drunkenness -** Over indulgence of alcohol or legal and illegal drugs for self- medicating or escapism purposes, resulting in intoxication.

Alcohol- intoxication (also known as **drunkenness** or **inebriation**) is a physiological state that occurs when a person has a high level of ethanol (alcohol) in his or her blood.

It is also known as getting smashed or drinking too much.

Scripture does not forbid the drinking of alcohol. But sternly warns against its over use.

The effects of strong drink are vividly described in the OT.

There are frequent references to the unsteady gait of drunkards.

Job 12:25; Ps 107:27; Isa 19:14;

They are prone to quarrelsomeness and brawling (*Prov 20:1; 23:19-*

When drinking their minds are confused, their understanding is taken away

(*Hos 4:11*); they neglect their duties (*Prov 31:4, 5*); they think they are

heroes (*Isa 5:22*); they end their days in poverty (*Prov 21:17; 23:20, 21*) and in woe and sorrow (*23:29-32*).

Alcohol and drugs are considered very similar. They both can be addicting and separate a person from God.

17.   **Revelries** - Regularly attending wild parties or celebrations. unrestrained merry making, jubilation, celebration, festivities.

The opposite is "self-control". The bible has a lot to say about self control. Self-control fortifies the inner man. It builds a wall of defense around him against destructive forces of evil. The pathetic tragedy of the physically strong man Samson was the result of his intemperance in sensual desires. His sexual love for ungodly women decreed his doom *Judg 14:2, 1 Cor 7:5*).

Self-control is essential for success in the pursuit of any worthy goal. "Every athlete exercises self-control in all things. They do it to receive a perishable wreath, but we are imperishable" (*1 Cor 9:25*).

Did you identify one or more of the above sin characteristics as being prevalent in your life? Please don't panic. You are very blessed, not condemned. You now know what you have to do. Remember that most of us have fell victim to one or more of the above sins, at one time or another. There is only One who was and is perfect. We are taking the inventory to discover is if any of these have become so entrenched in our being that they now define who we are.

It is time to take action. Start today. Write down on a piece of paper what you have discovered. Write down what your thoughts and feelings are about it. It's important that you not allow yourself to forget or rationalize this new revelation away. Your eternal soul could be at stake.

The important thing to hold unto is that now you know how the demonic is gaining access into your life. By removing the strongholds of the demonic that these sins of the flesh create, one can be set free and move down the path of living with a faith that truly will overcome.

None of the characteristics mentioned above are terminal. You can stop from participating in any of them. But most of them you will find that you may not be able to get out or stop on your own power. It may take an act of God to fix the situation. The phrase "I can't, there is One who can, so I am making a decision to ask and let Him", fits very well right here. Only the God of the universe, Jesus Christ, has the power to move mountains and make some of these major changes in our lives.

We may have to allow God to take away some things in our life that are very important to us or part of who we are. Some of this is going to hurt. But I guarantee you it will be just a temporary, small amount of pain, in exchange for an eternity of gain. The purpose isn't for you to simply change some things and gain a new purpose in your life. The purpose is to make sure you are included in the rapture and have an everlasting life with Jesus, the creator.

So-- we bring our troubles, faults and pains to the Lord.

Relax. He is faithful! He always listens and always responds! Ask the Lord to send the Holy Spirit to minister and help to you. He will be your strength!

1Th 5:6 Therefore let us not sleep as the rest do, but let us watch and be calm.

1Th 5:7 For those sleeping, sleep in the night, and those being drunken are drunken in the night.

1Th 5:8 But let us, who are of the day, be calm, having put on the breastplate of faith and love and the hope of salvation for a helmet.

1Th 5:9 For God has not appointed us to wrath, but to obtain salvation by our Lord Jesus Christ,

1Th 5:10 who died for us, so that whether we watch or sleep we should live together with Him.

1Th 5:11 Therefore comfort one another, and edify one another, even as you also do.

Examine yourself and trust Jesus Christ. He is here and waiting to cleanse and justify you right now. TODAY may be your day to make some changes. Let the power of God help you. We are powerless over so many things. He is the powerful one and can move mountains.

Make some decisions and become free.

Remember that:

Philippians 3:20 For our citizenship is in Heaven, from which also we are looking for the Savior, the Lord Jesus Christ,

3:21 who shall change our body of humiliation so that it may be fashioned like His glorious body, according to the working of His power, even to subdue all things to Himself.

1 Thessalonians 5:21 Test (Examine) all things, and hold firmly that which is good.

Print out this prayer. Pray about the prayer and then go to a quiet place and let what is in your heart come through your lips and up to the Lord. It's the salvation prayer. Watch the video below if you feel you need some coaching.

If you want to be assured eternal salvation today, just pray this simple prayer with sincerity, humility and from the bottom of your soul. Print it out and read it, if you need to. But mean it!

We go to a quiet place, humble ourselves before the creator of the universe, Jesus Christ, and pray:

"Dear Jesus, I believe in You. I believe You are the only Son of God and that You shed your blood and died for my sins, and that You were buried and rose again as it is written in the bible. I'm sorry for the things I've done that hurt You. Forgive me for all my sins Lord Jesus.

Come into my heart today, take charge of my life and make me the way You want me to be. With Your ever present help, I renounce all my sinful practices of the past. Cleanse my heart with Your precious Blood. I believe You are the creator and the only way to salvation. I surrender my will and my life to You. Fill me with your Holy Spirit. In Jesus Christ's Name I ask, Amen."

My friend, if you prayed that prayer and meant it from the bottom of your heart your eternal salvation is assured! You will never be alone again! Please make sure that you get baptized soon and receive the Holy Spirit. You are becoming part of something that is so special and that will be with you for the rest of your days. Your eternal destiny has just been assured. No amount of "good works" could do what you are doing! And the eternal gift is free! You can now live each and every day with *An Enduring Faith* that will help you to overcome.

Now, to make your days full of joy and freedom, study your bible daily. Start with the book of John in the New Testament. Let the Love of Jesus wash over you. We recommend using a verse memorization program. Place a verse on your heart every couple days or so. Be relentless. Place your will and your life into the Lord's care every morning and thank him every night.

Now, take a moment and thank the One who saved you from eternal destruction.

The Salvation Prayer (click here) is in the Joseph Plan Blog.

"God did not give us a spirit of timidity but a spirit of power and love and self-control" (*2 Tim 1:6, 7*)

John 15: 12-14 This is My commandment, that you love one another as I have loved you.

If you have a hard time dealing with any of your identified sins, natural bondage's or character issues, we strongly advise you to go see a bible believing pastor, Christian consular or a born again Christian you can pray with and share your burdens. All of them can be dealt with by surrendering them to the Lord. Only He is strong enough. It is getting there that we all need help with.

Living with any of the "Works of the Flesh" will keep you from true righteousness and short of the power and authority of Jesus Christ.

We serve a powerful God and He doesn't want any of us, especially you, to miss the big event or suffer from the attacks of the demonic.

May God Bless You and Keep You Safe!

Pastor Thomas Holm

http://www.thejosephplan.org

Do you have your copy of the manual? It is the course textbook. You need one to get the full this teaching series. You can get your copy at Kindle Books or at our little book store.

See: *http://www.thejosephplan.org/book-store/product/biblical-spiritual-warfare-manual/*

Lesson Five

Symptoms of Demonic Oppression

B Y WHOSE AUTHORITY can we be delivered?
Plus, the Thirteen Symptoms of Demonic Attack that DEMAND ACTION

By whose authority can we bind, loose and cast out ALL DEMONIC Influences and inflictions?

By whose authority can we say the deliverance prayer and truly be delivered from Evil Spirits, the Occult and evil thoughts, words or deeds?

By whose authority can we become free of the Devils Demons?

Do you believe that under the authority of Jesus Christ that the Spirit within you, the Holy Spirit, has the power to command the entire spirit world and they MUST obey?

This understanding is foundational for anyone to be a successful spiritual warrior and to be a spiritual overcomer in our daily battles with the demonic- WE MUST BELIEVE!

By whose authority can we say, "I rebuke you in the name of Jesus Christ", and know with confidence that the spirit within that person, place or thing has been rebuked?

To rebuke means to admonish or stop one in its tracks.

Can we say-"Under the authority of the Catholic church?" Or how about-"Under the authority of Pastor Susan or Pastor Thomas?" of course not! None of these have the authority to cast out anything within the spiritual world on their own.

BUT, In Christian spiritual warfare, when an evil spirit, disease, or evil person is commanded in the name of Jesus Christ, it is coming from the Jesus of the bible directly. The scriptures tell us that the name of Jesus Christ IS the Word of God. Therefore, when a demonic spirit is given a command in the name of Jesus Christ, you are using the fullest biblical definitions of God to defeat the demonic. You are throwing the entire Word of God at them.

It is important for us to be very clear which Jesus we are acknowledging as the creator, Lord and King over the entire universe. That might sound silly to some, but the enemy is very crafty and when it is given a command we must make sure that we don't give them any wiggle room because of the words we use.

Can the "higher power" of the world's agnostic religious system command such authority?

Can the Jesus of the Muslim religion make such a command and be obeyed?

Can the Jesus of the Book of Mormon make such a command and be obeyed?

When a Mormon, who is a strict follower of the Book of Mormon, speaks of Jesus it could not be more far removed from the real Jesus of the KJV Holy Bible. The Mormons carry the KJV Holy Bible to get their foot in the door to recruit unsuspecting Christians to read ANOTHER Testament they have of their different Mormon Jesus. The book of Mormon is the other gospel of the other Jesus of Joseph Smith. The Jesus invented by Joseph Smith for

Joseph's Mormon cult, is the first spirit child of Elohim, just as all humans, angels, and demons are spirit children of Elohim. Joseph Smith's Mormon Jesus became flesh through physical intercourse between Elohim, who Joseph Smith said has a physical body, to accomplish physically what he did with the Virgin Mary. That is the Mormon Jesus of Joseph Smith.

And this Joseph Smith has nothing in common with the Joseph of Genesis that is the name sake of this ministry.

The Mormon Jesus is the half-brother of Lucifer. The Mormon Jesus supposedly

came to earth to become a god. The sacrificial death of the Mormon Jesus is

supposed to give immortality to every creature, including animals at the Resurrection.

\According to Mormon doctrine whether an individual creature spends eternity confined to this earth, which is the Mormon definition of hell, or in one of three heavens, is totally up to his, her, or its, performance. The only way to heaven is by earning favor or blessings. This is not THE Gospel of the Jesus Christ of the Holy Bible, but the other gospel of Joseph Smith, about a Jesus imagined by Joseph Smith.

Can the Mormon Jesus take authority over all? Can a strict Lutheran or Catholic?

You, being a born again, saved, believer in Jesus Christ, have the authority to say:

"Under the authority of Jesus Christ and through the power of the Holy Ghost, I bind, break, loose and cast out of_____ all familiar and un-familiar evil spirits. Under the authority of Jesus Christ and the power of the Holy Ghost, I command you to leave (person, place or thing) NOW!"

Symptoms of possible demonic influence or attack

If you or a loved one have noticed a sudden physical or emotional change in your thinking or behavior, you may be under demonic influence or attack.

Demonic manifestations or influences can come about in many forms and for many reasons. When they happen they can be disruptive and possibly harmful. Satan is our enemy. He will use any opening we give Him. The purpose of this teaching is to help you understand if Satan and his helpers have gained access and are causing problems in your life. It isn't a complete inventory or assessment.

First of all, the devil hates Christians and he will do anything within his power to ruin our testimony. He is the great deceiver and the great tempter. He will use any one at any time to try and destroy us. But, if you are a saved Christian always remember, if you have the right tools the spirit within you is more powerful than anything the demonic can throw against you,.

You don't have to be oppressed by sin and the demonic. You can live in peace.

Sin being allowed to gain a stronghold in our life is the most common cause for demonic attack. Any Christian can come under attack by demonic forces. Any repetitive sin in our life is an opening for a demonic stronghold to take hold and become fertile ground for the devil. Honest repentance should rid a Christian of these unwanted pests.

Sin in our life is the primary reason why the demonic can take a hold of us and try to influence us.

Certain anti or non-Christian activities we can involve ourselves in can also be a direct cause. We may get involved with them for seemingly good reasons. But the results of contrary or non-biblical activities can be harmful and even devastating. They can sometimes be just as devastating as indirect satanic involvement.

Demons are real. We have to face the fact that the spiritual world does contain demonic beings. And they are not your friends. They want you sick, confused, fearful, angry, not in the Word, isolated and maybe dead. For sure they do not want you worshiping the one true God. They don't want you in true worship to Jesus Christ, the Jesus Christ of the bible. The only One through which we can be saved and free to live with Agape love and in peace.

As stated above, two of the ways the demonic can take hold or influence a person is through repetitive, unrepentant sin or through an activity that opens a doorway for the demonic to come in. Drug abuse is an example of this. There are many others, like the idol worship of Buddha or the adoption of non-Christian tenants and bringing them into our faith. We will be discussing additional doorways or reasons in a later chapter.

Below is a list of symptoms that I hope you will pay particular attention too. It is what I call the Big Thirteen Symptoms

The following is only a partial list of the symptoms of demonic influence and attack. There are many spiritual powers. This list represents the primary culprits we should be aware of. By examining them you should be able to get a sense if you or your loved one is being affected by them. I encourage you to consider them thoughtfully and prayerfully. Any one of them may be a reason for concern.

But there may be medical causes connected to them. Real cellular medical issues that need the attention of your doctor may be present. Be cautious when examining this list. I advise you to talk this over with another Christian before putting a label of some kind on the situation. In the Biblical Spiritual Warfare Manual you are being given the tools you will need to break the hold any spirit may have on your life or your household. When one suffers from multiple symptoms then we can be relatively confident that the demonic is involved. That usually is proof positive that we are dealing with demonic oppression.

There are many reasons or possible causes of demonic attacks. The person being attacked may be involved in some sort of activity that is allowing or inviting the spiritual negativity in. It may be caused by someone close to you that may be opening a spiritual doorway. It also could be the result of a demonic curse or jinx of some sort. We'll cover many of the possible causes in the manual and also provide lists of symptoms and the names of different spiritual entities that are out there.

The below list is a partial list of changes in behavior or thinking that can occur after one has started or been involved in an activity that opens Satan's doorway. But we should also understand that these same symptoms may have a medical cause. If any of these are particularly bothersome, controlling or persistent it is always recommended that you see a medical doctor.

First, here is a general list of some of the symptoms of demonic oppression.

The following are symptoms that might indicate the presence or influence of any demonic entity. This list should be used as a general guide only. There are many of articles on this subject in the Spiritual Warfare category.

(Not possession for a Christian! A saved Christian cannot be possessed in the terms and how the secular world thinks or uses the word.)

* Thinking thoughts "that are not you."

* Having sudden depression.

* Having fits of anger that are unusual for you.

* Feeling hopeless.

* Your pets start acting differently around you.

* Your close friends start questioning your thinking or behavior.

* Excessive fatigue.

Symptoms of demonic control or attack:

* Not being able to do what you know is good or right.

* Feeling like you are being pulled to do the wrong thing.

* Feeling like you are being pressured to do something you don't want to do.

* Hearing voices or thoughts in your head that are negative, persuasive, or commanding you to do something.

* Deep or severe personality changes like fear or wanting to be isolated all the time.

- Suddenly having creepy or scary feelings.

- Recent feelings that an area, like in your house, there is something heavy, depressive or oppressive.

- Feelings of being under attack or threatened when others don't.

- Finding it hard or impossible to pray.

- Finding it harder or impossible to spend time with Christian brothers or sisters.

- Sudden and unexplainable anxiety.

- Sudden development of Lupus or other auto immune system disease.

If you have just one of the above symptoms it could be caused by many things and we do not want you to get alarmed. Some medical conditions can cause similar conditions. It could be from a new bad habit or an encounter with a sinful situation or circumstance. If this is true, Repent, make the appropriate changes and move on with your life. Trust in Jesus. If you keep experiencing them after doing the spiritual work, then consider Deliverance.

If you are experiencing or have identified multiple symptoms from the above list or if one of these symptoms is causing severe problems, it is most likely time to take action. You are very possibly under a demonic influence or attack. Most of these attacks occur from sin in our lives, life style issues or incorrect teachings. All of these can be dealt with so that you are free from the evil thoughts or influences. But they must be dealt with. Repentance is the answer to our own sin and self-deliverance warfare works much of the time. Always do it first and as soon as possible. Please refer to your Biblical Spiritual Warfare Manual.

Please remember to consult your doctor to make sure there aren't any physical or serious mental or emotional issues that need medical attention.

There is another category of demonic attack that we need to be aware of. If the symptoms started AFTER you started practicing a new type of meditation or any other non-biblical activity I encourage you to address the issue immediately. Stop doing what you are doing NOW. Eastern meditation is a New Age Fad that has swept through thousands of churches. It is one of the most popular fads of the new millennium, within the Christian church community.

There are known relationships between eastern or non-biblical meditation and demonic influence. The proponents don't tell us about these. You are going to want to see your pastor, of course. But before you start making appointments, I would recommend that you bring this to the Lord in prayer and visit with a trusted Christian friend about it. Have both of you open up your bible and do some research. Pray together and seek the truth.

Eastern Meditation techniques are Non-Christian (anti) and are always an open door for the demonic. It doesn't matter if the session or words are book ended with the name of Jesus.

If it was your pastor that got you involved in this activity you may want to bring a Christian friend with you to discuss it with the pastor. He or she may not know the great negatives that are present in these types of activities. Although you need to know that some major denominations are endorsing such practices. Pray for the pastor before you meet with him or her. Pray that the Lord pours out His spirit of truth and wisdom upon them. Bring your bible to the meeting and ask the pastor to show you what the Word of God says about the activity in question. In this final age in which we live, we cannot afford to be placing our trust on the wisdom of man or a faddy non-Christian program that is outside of God's Word. We need the truth and guidance of the Word. The Eternal Word! Many souls are depending on it.

If you answered one of the above symptoms in the positive it isn't necessarily a demonic attack. It is possibly a sin in your life or a false teaching that needs addressing. However, it may be. Prayer and discernment are going to have to be relied on. If you have two or more of the listed symptoms I would strongly suggest that you get some "bible based" spiritual warfare and deliverance help. You will find many pages and chapters dealing with this in the Biblical Spiritual Warfare Manual. If you don't have your copy yet, I give them away free to all those who can't afford one. Just write me and provide a short explanation.

In prayer and under the authority of Jesus Christ the demonic must flee as Jesus leads us and reveals the truth. If you find yourself unable to pray right about this or if you believe it is severe enough of a problem- get some help. Call a Christian prayer partner.

Contact a Christian minister who has real life experience in spiritual warfare, if you can find one. For extreme situations we are in the process of developing a list or network of seasoned Deliverance ministries that you may contact.

When commanded by the authority of Jesus Christ and the power of the Holy Ghost the demonic MUST flee. Praying for forgiveness through repentance, in the name of Jesus Christ should rid a believer of any of these. If you are a saved Christian, not simply a church member or pew sitter Christian, you have the spiritual authority, in God's world, to command the demonic to leave. Pray often. Pray earnestly. Immerse yourself in the Word of God.

There are symptoms that we can all be aware of that always should be addressed with deliverance.

The Thirteen Symptoms of Demonic Attack that DEMAND ACTION.

If you or a loved one has any one of the following symptoms of a Demonic attack, it is strongly suggested that you take action as soon as possible. The demonic wants us sick, in rebellion to God and most of all dead and eternally separated from Him.

Below is a list of physical or emotional symptoms or manifestations that can often be noticed by changes in ones thinking or behavior. They almost assuredly are caused by a demonic attack.

If one is identified, call your doctor and make an appointment and then start spiritual warfare now.

Please don't sit around waiting for the situation to improve on its own. If one of the following symptoms is seriously present-- it is ALERT time, especially if they worsen or seem critically intense. They are symptoms of a problem that should be addressed immediately.

The following symptoms are always related to demonic influence of some kind. In general, the stronger the symptom the more control the demonic has on one's life. The following should not be taken lightly. Any one of them could be very serious, some even dangerous. But I want to assure you, that in each case God has provided us with a solution. If you identify yourself or a loved one as suffering from one of the following symptoms it is time to get into action.

You don't have to suffer any more. You don't have to be a victim of the spiritual world. As you are learning, there is an answer in Biblical teachings that will give you the tools to overcome. In chapter six you are provided a list of many of the spirits the enemy throws at us, all demonic spirits that can cause these problems.

If you identify one of the following listed symptoms as being part of your life please refer directly to chapter ten of the manual, which is the chapter on Deliverance from the demonic. If you can I suggest you have a trusted Christian friend help you and preferably a trained member of the Christian clergy to guide and assist you.

There is more power through prayer when it is done by two or more. Please follow the instructions and be assured. A lot of hours and experience went into the material in chapters 7-11 of the Biblical Spiritual Warfare Manual. Please read, pray about and follow the suggested courses of action. There is way too much material to reproduce here. Through God all things are possible and by His power all demonic MUST OBEY!

Here is the list of the Thirteen Symptoms of Demonic Attack. This specific list is not in your manual, but will be included and expanded upon in the next edition. When one or more of the following symptoms is present I always recommend Spiritual Warfare and Deliverance.

1. Compulsive and uncontrollable urge to blaspheme God

2.   Rage-Sudden and unexplained outbursts of uncontrollable rage

3.   Seizures of Anxiety that can almost paralyze you. Gripping anxiety that is unjustified

4.   Compulsive thoughts of suicide or murder (contact emergency services immediately)

5.   Numbing feeling of Guilt when you haven't done anything wrong

6.   Severe, non-medicine related, sudden Depression

7.   Terrifying doubt of one's assurance of Salvation

8.   Perverted or obsessed sexual desires

9.   Nightmares and dreams that cause severe anxiety, fear or anger

10. Abuse. Irrational compulsion to hurt or mutilate yourself or others

11. Un-explainable contortions of the body

12. Aversions or violent reactions to the Blood of Jesus or hearing the Gospel.

13. Gripping or paralyzing Fear, that is unjustified and/or irrational.

A big clue of a severe demonic presence is if your pet starts acting differently around you or the person in question. Many animals have a sixth sense that can be very sensitive to the spiritual world.

Refer to chapters nine through eleven for a more complete list of symptoms and the different spirits that can affect us, along with the prayers to use to overcome and to be free forever of them.

The next lesson will be concentrated on Deliverance. It will be from a slightly different perspective than is contained in the manual.

If you find that you have been providing access to the demonic, you should take immediate steps to correct it. Remember, the God we worship is greater than all other spiritual entities out there. Jesus Christ is the most powerful name in the universe and under His covering and protection you will always be kept safe. There is no need to panic. Prayer by a believer conquers all.

There are very powerful prayers contained in the "Biblical Spiritual Warfare Manual" that give you the spiritual tools to overcome the demonic and be one of us that "endures until the end" (Matt 24). Yes, this is a problem that throughout history the Lord has dealt with. If You Believe, pray the Spiritual Warfare Prayers and stop doing the activities that allowed them in, these symptoms should subside soon. You are in our prayers.

Ephesians 1:17 That the God of our Lord Jesus Christ, the Father of glory, may give unto you the spirit of wisdom and revelation in the knowledge of him:

Ephesians 1:19 And what [is] the exceeding greatness of his power to us-ward who believe, according to the working of his mighty power.

Once again, if any of the symptoms listed above are extreme or threatening to you or others-Call your doctor and confer with a Christian spiritual warfare minister immediately and pray together for the Blood of Jesus to intercede, protect and to give you wisdom and direction. .

You may also like to check out the "Break the Bondage of Fear" ebook. It is a complete Christian resource, which will show you how to live your life free of all fear. The "Break the Bondage of Fear" ebook" by Pastor Thomas. It is a spiritual warfare book that has been read and used by Christians all over the world.

You will want to have read up through chapter twelve in the manual before the next lesson.

Lesson Six

Deliverance from all Demonic

Deliverance Prayer- To rid yourself of evil spirits, curses or demonic influences

Deliverance from the strongholds of sin!

ONE OF THE FREE GIFTS OF JESUS is deliverance from the stronghold of sin!

Remember the saying that possession is nine tenths of the law. That is a general rule of law in society. In spiritual warfare possession is 100% of the law. If we are complacent and allow the demonic to remain in a certain part of our life, we are giving the devil legal permission to operate within our lives! Because, in spite of our supposed righteousness, the devil still has a stronghold.

A stronghold is a base of operations for the demonic. The natural spirit centers in our mind and our mind will become a house of wrong thinking or a fortress of bad thoughts or ideas. We get them from our natural self-will, the examples of our parents, society and from bad teachers.

A stronghold of sin occurs when our thinking develops a bad habit, attitude or a belief that is contrary to God's will and Word. Through our thinking or non-thinking we give that sinful habit, situation or attitude permission to be present in our life. Once we accept sin as part of who we are we have given the demonic permission to operate from their new stronghold on us. The evil one has established a base of operation.

Because He gave us free choice, God allows this to happen.

2Co 10:3 For though walking about in flesh, we do not war according to flesh.

2Co 10:4 For the weapons of our warfare are not fleshly, but mighty through God to the pulling down of strongholds,

2Co 10:5 pulling down imaginations and every high thing that God allow this to happen exalts itself against the knowledge of God, and bringing into captivity every thought into the obedience of Christ;

2Co 10:6 and having readiness to avenge all disobedience, when your obedience is fulfilled.

2Co 10:7 do you look at things according to appearance? If anyone has persuaded himself that he is Christ's, let him think this again as to himself, that as he is Christ's, even so we are Christ's.

Spiritual Strongholds are sins, ideas or attitudes that get us into a place of spiritual bondage or slavery to the evil one's ways. When we have a spiritual stronghold, we are slaves and in Bondage to sin, Spiritual Bondage.

We can get into bondage to the:

Spirit of Fear- Yes, we can be slaves to fear.

Spirit of Pride

Spirit of Anger

Spirit of Rage

Spirit of Resentments

Spirit of Greed

Spirit of Sexual Gratification

Spirit of Sexual Perversion

Spirit of Materialism

Spirit of Laziness

Refer to your textbook for a much more complete list. They can also be defined as anything that exalts itself above our relationship with Jesus Christ/God.

Spiritual Strongholds are also human reasoning's that exalt themselves over the revelation of God's will for our lives as revealed in Scripture.

One of the primary sources of us developing strongholds is because of society's religion of Agnosticism.

It can be summarized by: "I am a god "and "If we think it, we can create it and do it!" It includes the idea that we or I can reason our way into peace, comfort, love and well-being. The problem we all get into is that we can, maybe with all good intentions, reason our way into a thinking or action that is outside of God's will. When we do that and accept it as part our life style, we have formed a Stronghold from which the demonic can operate. We have made the choice to give the demonic legal authority to mess with our lives, brains and actions. Whether we understand it at the time or not!

It should be all of ours goal to get free of that Bondage.

God made spiritual rules for our lives and when we violate them, there are consequences. Whether good intended or not. Unfortunately, many of us do not realize that we have gotten ourselves into that position until we are suffering the consequences.

Through Jesus Christ and the Word of God we can be free of all of the demonic Strongholds in our life and become a slave to righteousness and God's ways.

John 8:32 And you shall know the truth, and the truth shall make you free.

John 8:36 So if the Son sets you free, you will be free indeed.

John 1:14 The Word became flesh and made his dwelling among us. We have seen his glory, the glory of the one and only Son, who came from the Father, full of grace and truth.

Romans 6:18You have been set free from sin and have become slaves to righteousness.

Jesus came here to set us free. Free of sin and its resulting Strongholds. Only He through His blood has the power to cleanse us of this sin.

1 Corinthians 7:22 For the one who was a slave when called to faith in the Lord is the Lord's freed person; similarly, the one who was free when called is Christ's slave.

2 Corinthians 3:17 Now the Lord is the Spirit, and where the Spirit of the Lord is, there is freedom.

Galatians 5:1 It is for freedom that Christ has set us free. Stand firm, then, and do not let yourselves be burdened again by a yoke of slavery (bondage).

There is a wonderful passage in Scripture that demonstrates how to use the Word of God in prayer, to demolish the strongholds in your life.

It is James 4:7-10

James 4:7Therefore submit yourselves to God. Resist the devil, and he will flee from you.

James 4:8 Draw near to God, and He will draw near to you. Cleanse your hands, sinners; and purify your hearts, double-minded ones.

James 4:9 Be afflicted, and mourn and weep. Let your laughter be turned to mourning and your joy to heaviness

James 4:10 Be humbled before the Lord, and He will lift you up.

These passages identify the four steps we should take to defeat the devil's work in our life. They are a pattern to use to do deliverance and spiritual warfare. It also gives us two promises that will happen in our life if we do.

We should use the Word's teachings in prayer as our primary tool for submitting to God and conquering the enemy and any of his strongholds.

James says," Submit yourselves to God." We acknowledge from God's Word that Jesus is Lord (see Romans 10:9

To be spiritually cleansed, we go to God in prayer. It is instructive and so very powerful. James writes, "Wash your hands, you sinners, and purify your hearts, you double-minded."

We acknowledge that the Blood of Jesus cleanses us from sin (John1:7) Draw near to God by reading and studying His Word.

James instructs us, "Cleanse your hands, sinners; and purify your hearts" We ask God the Father to draw us near and cleanse us. In order for that to happen we must be totally willing. (John 6:44.)

Then we enter with confidence into His Holy Place (see Hebrews 4:16) Stand against Satan's temptations with God's Word.

James commands us to resist the devil.

We expose Satan's lies with the truth of God's Word (Hebrews 4:12) and exercise our authority over him by commanding him and taking back our ground. (Matthew 16:33.)

God's promise through this passage in James is that when we take these four steps of submitting to God, two things will happen.

Promises He makes to each of us.

1- God will "come near to [us]"

2- Satan will "flee from [us-with the Holy Spirit]."

The promises are that our relationship with God will be strong and the strongholds that Satan had in our lives will be destroyed. Satan fleeing from us is the same as sin fleeing from us.

In the hands of a true believer, with a repentant and surrendered heart, one can truly see the strongholds of sin will be moved out of the way. The enemy moved back. Victory over evil claimed

2Co 10:3 For though walking about in flesh, we do not war according to flesh.

2Co 10:4 For the weapons of our warfare are not fleshly, but mighty through God to the pulling down of strongholds,

2Co 10:5 pulling down imaginations and every high thing that exalts itself against the knowledge of God, and bringing into captivity every thought into the obedience of Christ;

2Co 10:6 and having readiness to avenge all disobedience, when your obedience is fulfilled.

2Co 10:7 Do you look at things according to appearance? If anyone has persuaded himself that he is Christ's, let him think this again as to himself, that as he is Christ's, even so we are Christ's.

Jesus came here to set us free. Free us of sin and its resulting Strongholds. Only He has the power to cleanse us of this sin.

Romans 8:2 because through Christ Jesus the law of the Spirit who gives life has set you free from the law of sin and death.

Here is a sample Deliverance prayer. We have a number of them in the "Biblical Spiritual Warfare Manual". This is a short version, but it will give you a good idea what a Deliverance prayer should contain.

In it we are declaring that God is God and that we are not. We are recognizing His authority over all evil and beseeching Him to take the righteous action of cleansing and purifying our lives.

In the hands of a true believer, with a repentant and surrendered heart, one can truly see the strongholds of sin by moved out of the way. The enemy moved back. Victory over evil claimed.

PRAYER FOR DELIVERANCE

"In the name of the Lord Jesus Christ I pray. Lord Jesus, You are all powerful, only You are fully God! I beseech You for the deliverance of (myself) or (our brothers and sisters names) who are enslaved by the evil one.

I beseech you Lord Jesus to free me (or?) from all anxiety, sadness, and obsessions. I beg You Lord-Free me O Lord. Break my bondage from all hatred, fornication, envy. Free me, O Lord, from thoughts of jealousy, rage, and death. Free us (me), O Lord from every thought of suicide and physical harm. I beg You Lord to free us from every form of sinful sexuality. Free us Lord, from every division in our family, and every harmful friendship. Free us Lord, from every sort of spell, curse, witchcraft, and from every form of the occult activity.

We beg You: Free us, O Lord. Break our (my) bondage.

I repent of (name the sin(s) of (_____) and declare that I am willing to have you change me.

Lord Jesus, it is You who said, "I leave you peace, my peace I give you," through the power of the Holy Ghost of God, we may be liberated from every evil spirit and enjoy Your peace always.

In the name of Jesus Christ, Yeshua. Amen.

There is a spiritual war going on and all of us are feeling the effects. None of us are immune from the demonic that is rising all around us. This ministry is here to pronounce to all that we need not be the victims in this spiritual battle. With the proper knowledge and tools we can all be Overcomers over the evil that is rising.

Whether your battle is with the enemy around you or the enemy within, there is help in God's word. There are lessons we can all use to be Overcomers in this war for our souls and lives.

If your battle is from within we offer you a solution. God provides us with answers. What is sad is how few of us have received the proper teachings.

If you are in a personal battle with the evil one, the prayer of Deliverance is your solution. I invite you to study it and try to understand its significance. It is not new, although if you have only been taught by a modern denominational church, the odds are you may never have heard of it. I want to assure you that this is solid teaching for every Christian. It is 100% biblically based. It has been used for centuries and is being used by millions of us today. It is probably the most effective prayer I am aware of to rid yourself of all demonic spirits that may have been given permission to enter your life. It can be used by all born again Christians. Although in order for it to be the most effective you may want a prayer partner and you must be sincere and mean the words that you pray.

The Deliverance prayer is a very powerful prayer. Many of us are in need of deliverance, at one time in our lives or another. Deliverance should be a foundational teaching for our spiritual walk and our overall health.

If in your past or your families past, you have had familiar contact or personally interacted with anyone or anything that was demonically influenced; you could be under a demonic oppression. This prayer can be prayed to rid and free you from all past and present sinful or evil relationships. Regardless of how innocent they may have seemed at the time.

It is important to remember that the Blood of Jesus and what He accomplished for us on the cross is powerful enough to wash us from all past and present sin. We must repent however and accept His forgiveness. I offer this prayer to everyone as a primary tool for your spiritual warfare tool box. It will provide total protection and covering.

Read it through a few times before you try to offer it in prayer. But I wouldn't try to second guess the wordage too much. Feel free to omit the parts that you are positive do not apply to you. But be a little careful, sometimes we have associated with occult practices and people or demonic activities and not even know or remembered it.

We consider this prayer and the pleading of the Blood of Jesus to be foundational in our spiritual battle during these end times. The battle is evident; many of us are under attack. These teachings and prayers can be our greatest defense.

The "Biblical Spiritual Warfare Manual", should be kept handy for use any time in the future. It contains everything you will need to protect yourself and defeat the enemy.

How to pray for Freedom from all, demonic oppression, receive Deliverance and how and why to pray the Blood of Jesus Prayer. These topics and much more are covered.

Before you start using this prayer I recommend you first examine yourself and take a simple inventory. This prayer, as with many others, will work better when we are in the proper spiritual position with the Lord. Anyone can say this prayer and it will always deliver some level of relief. The Word helps us here.

This prayer is the most effective when one is in surrender or submission to God and His ways. For this prayer to be the most powerful and effective one should be in a "positional authority" under Jesus. In other words totally believe from your heart that only He is the One True God and that you aren't. Your heart should be in a state of repentance and a thorough examination of oneself and your actions should be done before you use it. The spiritual health checklist request form, located at the end of the manual, should actually be the first thing one does when learning spiritual warfare. Every Christian needs to get their house in order before going into battle. We have prepared a helpful report on spiritual conditioning. I strongly advise you to study the "Rapture ForeWarning Advisory" above and do a thorough examination of yourself ASAP.

Use it to determine if your house is in order. This report is for all those seeking to become free through an enduring relationship with the Lord Jesus. I encourage you to not skip this part. A healthy, positional relationship with the Lord is the solid ground upon which we stand when conducting spiritual warfare. Although some of us need to pray the Deliverance prayer first in order to clean house. You will have to decide.

In the hands of any honest person, with a repentant and surrendered heart, one can truly see the mountains are moved. The enemy moved back. Victory over evil claimed. I guarantee you -- that YOU ARE NOT THE EXCEPTION to God's love and protection.

Here is a longer version of the Deliverance Prayer. Take the time to "examine yourself" and personalize it before using it. Personal repentance and deliverance through this prayer and the power of the Blood of Jesus will free you. There are those of us, however, that I strongly recommend the help of a trusted prayer partner or minister to accomplish deliverance. You be the judge.

"SELF DELIVERANCE" AND "FREEDOM" FROM

THE BONDAGE OF EVIL SPIRITS!

Repeat the following prayer loudly to be delivered from the occult, evil spirits and evil thoughts, words or deeds. Use the parts that pertain to you. Remembering always that it is God working within and through you that is able to do this. On our own we are powerless!

Thank you Lord Jesus for dying for my sins, thank you for your glorious resurrection and for making me a new person through faith in your precious blood.

Dear Lord, I confess that in the past through ignorance, curiosity, foolishness or willfulness, I have disobeyed your Word. I now ask you to help me as I renounce all those things. Lord cleanse me in body, mind, soul and spirit. Satan, I am closing any door which I may have opened to you and your demons through contacts with the occult.

Under the authority of Jesus Christ and by the power of the Holy Ghost, I renounce and rebuke all contacts or any involvement with Satan, Satanism, black mass and demon worship.(See the two chapters in the manual- "The authority of Jesus Christ.)

I renounce and rebuke all contacts with Witchcraft, White Magic, Black Magic, Voodoo, Dungeons & Dragons (used for advanced training of witches), Spiritualist, Black Mass, Ouija boards and other occult games.

I renounce and rebuke all kinds of fortune telling, tea leaf reading, coffee ground reading, palm reading (Chiromancy), crystal balls, Contumacy (tarot and other card) playing, all dependency on astrology, biorhythm and feedback, Irisology (fortune telling by the iris of the eye), birth signs and horoscopes, spirit guides or counselors, pendulum swinging, false cults and wearing charm earrings.

I renounce and rebuke all water witching or dowsing, levitation, body-lifting, table tipping, automatic handwriting and handwriting analysis.

I renounce and rebuke all Psychometric (divination through objects), Geomancy, Promancy, Aeromancy, Arithmancy, Capnomancy, Rhapsodmancy, Phrenology (fortune telling by bumps on the head) and Augury that are part of fortune telling.

I renounce and rebuke the heresy of reincarnation and all healing groups involved in metaphysics and spiritualism.

I do renounce and rebuke every psychic and occult contact that I have had.

I renounce and rebuke all kind of hypnosis, self-hypnosis under any excuse or authority.

I renounce and rebuke all transcendental meditation, yoga, Zen, all eastern cults and religions, mysticism, idol worship and false religions.

I renounce and rebuke every cult that denies the blood of Jesus Christ and every philosophy which denies the Divinity of the Lord Jesus and the Trinity. Lord I confess the sin of seeking from self or Satan the help that should have only come from God. I confess as sin (name all occult contacts and occult sins committed) and also those occult sins I cannot remember.

I renounce and rebuke all psychic heredity that I may have had and break any demonic hold and curses over myself and my family line back to Adam and Eve on both sides of my parents through the power of the blood of the Lord Jesus Christ.

I renounce and rebuke all forms of the martial arts, including judo, Kung fu, and Karate.

I renounce and rebuke all literature I have ever read and studied in all of these fields and I will destroy such books in my possession.

Lord I now repent and renounce and rebuke all those sins and ask you to forgive me

(1John 1:9). I renounce Satan and all his works. I count them as my enemies. I now close the door to all practices and command all such spirits to leave me in the mighty name of Jesus Christ.

I renounce and rebuke the Prince of Occult Sex and all the sex spirits which entered through the occult involvement, eyes, participation, transfer or by inheritance and command all of his demons to come out of the sex organs, the lips, tongue, the taste buds, throat, and mind in the name of Jesus Christ my Savior.

Heavenly Father, I come to you in the name of the Lord Jesus Christ. I believe that he is the Son of God who takes away the sin of all those who repent and confess him as Lord. I believe that the blood of Jesus Christ cleanses me from all sin. I claim freedom from all filth which has come through my eyes, my ears, my mind or through actual participation in sin. In particular, I confess the following: all preoccupation with sensual desire and appetites, and indulgences of them; all longing and ardent desire for what is forbidden; all inordinate affection, all unnatural and unrestrained passions and lusts; the promoting or partaking of these which produce lewd emotion and foster sexual sin and lust.

In the name of Jesus Christ, I now rebuke, bind, break and loose myself and my family from any and all evil curses, fetishes, charms, love potions all psychic powers, sorcery, bewitchments, enchantments, hexes, spells, every jinx, and psychic prayers which have been put upon us, from both sides of generations of my father and mother back to Adam and Eve.

I bind, break and loose myself from any connected or related spirits from any person or persons or from any occult or psychic source.

I hereby reclaim all ground that I have ever given to Satan in body, mind, soul, or spirit. I dedicate myself to you Dear Lord, to be used for Your glory alone. I want You to control and empower every area of my life, including all my emotions; including my sexual powers; that from now on that I might be used according to your will. I also now give to You my affections, emotions and desires, and request that they might be motivated and controlled by Your Holy

Spirit. I hereby claim, total victory and freedom from all my former bondages.

I place myself, my family and our possessions under the covering of The Blood of Jesus Christ.

In Jesus Christ' name, Jeshua I ask. - Amen.

Repent of any sin in your life and place yourself under The Blood of Jesus for protection. Walk confidently in the freedom and victory that only Christ provides. He, by the shedding of His precious Blood has done it all for you. You have just claimed what our precious Lord and Savior has so freely given to you!

Amen! Amen! **Amen!** Rejoice!!

The most powerful prayer one can say!

Before we leave this lesson I want to give you a word of caution. Whenever a person has had spiritual warfare prayers prayed over them, the demonic has been super energized. They may have been just kicked out of the house they have been occupied for a long time or they may have just lost the stronghold from which they worked and thus lost their power.

They aren't going to take it lightly. They will do everything they can to win back their old home. So expect a spiritual battle for a few days.

The answer is to spend the next few hours after the warfare prayer time in prayer, praise and reading the Word of God. By doing so we are filling the spiritual space or house that was just cleaned.

For the next few days or a week please be very diligent about this. We must put our guard up and do our part with the Lord.

The warning-If we leave our house empty of the spirit, the biblical principle is that the demonic can come back in with up to seven times the number of his buddies and more powerful. I have personally witnessed this and it is very sad.

Why didn't this person do what was suggested to them? Only God knows!

I would also like to point out that you are not responsible for the results of any Deliverance or spiritual warfare session. It is God's job and He gets all the glory. If we take the credit we would also take the blame. This is only about God reclaiming what He wills.

God Bless and May the God of all creation keep you safe until then.

Pastor Thomas

Lesson Seven

How and Why to Plead the Blood

How, when and why to Plead the Blood of Jesus prayer.

MUCH OF THIS LESSON is taken directly out of both of my spiritual warfare books, especially out of chapter nine in the manual. There is not a lot of good solid teaching on this topic available, in my opinion. Most denominational churches stay away from it completely.

The "Blood of Jesus" is one of the most powerful prayers one can pray. It carries with it the entire force and command of the Gospel and the full power of the Spirit of God. It will become one of your most treasured and rewarding prayers you can say. If you learn to pray this prayer you will, in a very short time, be amazed watching what the Lord does, right in front of your eyes. You will be watching miracles happen and the powers of darkness flee from the presence and authority of God.

I understand that this has been an over powering teaching for many. It was written for those with an honest desire to learn Spiritual Warfare in depth. This is not a 101 course, more post graduate. As in so many challenges in one's life, all we can do is to do our best and put our trust in the Lord for the results. Take what you can and leave the rest until the Lord brings us up a step and opens our eyes to what we need to learn. That is part of what can make each new day exciting. I've been tuned in to this topic for over fifteen years now and there is still so much for me to learn.

This is a basic primary defensive weapon. A supreme prayer of protection.

This lesson is on How and Why to plead and pray "The Blood of Jesus Prayer".

I invite you to learn this prayer and to start using it TODAY. It is the most powerful prayer of protection available to a born again Christian! Used by millions around the world.

Here is a sample prayer on how to Plead the Blood of Jesus ON and OVER whatever you want God to protect. Our example is of a woman pleading to God the Father to protect her husband as he goes off to work. We can change the ON and FOR to meet the day's challenges and circumstances.

Heavenly Father. In the name of Jesus Christ and under His Authority I Plead the Blood of Jesus ON my husband and all that he does today.

I plead the Blood of Jesus FOR his protection and care.

I plead the Blood of Jesus FOR his protection against all familiar and unfamiliar spirits.

I plead the Blood of Jesus FOR his safe travel today and FOR safe delivery to his place of work.

I plead the Blood on his truck (car), his tools and all the people and equipment he will come into contact with today and for his safe return home.

Father I believe in you and have full faith and trust that the power and authority of your Sons precious Blood that He shed for us, will provide this protection.

In the name of your Son Jesus Christ, Jeshua, I pray.

AMEN

Place the basics of this prayer on your heart. Memorize it and incorporate it into your daily life. You may want to write it onto a 3 x 5 note card and use that as practice.

There are many reasons and situations when we can use this prayer. It can be said as often as you feel necessary.

I suggest you say this prayer as part of your normal Morning Prayer routine. Pray for the protection of the Blood ON yourself and ON all of your family and loved ones FOR protection and safety.

Pray and Plead the Blood of Jesus on:

1. Your house

2. Your car and travel

3. Your finances

4. Your work

5. You-Your body, soul and spirit, spouse, children and other loved ones

First - This prayer of protection can be said by anyone. But it won't be as effective as when said by a true believer, a born again Christian! One should be a saved, born again, filled with the Holy Spirit Christian to use this prayer to realize its maximum potential. With the assurance of salvation comes an increase in justification and authority to use this prayer and the spiritual power to direct it.

Second - In order for this prayer to be the most effective, the believer should be in a position of surrender or submission to God and His ways. It is called positional authority. The believer's heart should be in a state of repentance and a thorough examination of oneself should have been done before you attempt to use it.

It is God, through the Holy Spirit, that is doing all the work here. So please don't get hung up on self-examining yourself every time you say this prayer. That just needed to be said for your understanding.

'Not by might, nor by power, but by My Spirit,' says the Lord of hosts. (Zechariah 4:6)

Acts 1:8 "But you shall receive POWER when the Holy Spirit has come upon you; and you shall be witnesses to Me in Jerusalem, and in all Judea and Samaria, and to the end of the earth."

1 Thessalonians 1:5 "For our gospel did not come to you in word only, but also in POWER, and in the Holy Spirit ..."

1 Corinthians 4:20 "For the kingdom of God is not in word but in POWER.

A Spiritual Warfare and "Power of the Blood" story by Thomas.

I have personally witnessed the effectiveness of "The Blood of Jesus Prayer" many, many times and corresponded with hundreds of people around the world about it.

There are various reasons why we use this prayer.

The following story is one of many I could tell. It is a very interesting example of the utter power contained in this prayer. Yes, Jesus can and will, when called upon. On this particular day I had been home all day trying to do some writing and God had put it on my heart to include it in my prayers.

In 2005 I was full time in the ministry and living in a mobile home. I had taken in a homeless fellow for a few weeks. One night I was at my desk writing, with my back to the sliding glass door that went out to a patio. This fellow was walking through the study where I was working. As he walked by, he came to an abrupt halt and I looked up at him. He was stopped in his tracks and just standing there, with his mouth hanging open. Eyes wide open, pointing at the door behind me.

I swiveled my desk chair around to take a look and to my surprise I was looking right at a young man on the patio, standing up against the sliding screen door with his right arm raised to the side. Frozen! In his raised hand he was holding a carving knife and was standing in an attack mode.

I'm sure my jaw dropped as I got my cane to fend him off. But for a time he didn't move. He was honestly frozen. Then, two-three seconds later, he shook his head and his eyes opened wide, looking spooked. He stared right at me, dropped the knife and just turned and ran. The fellow that was staying with me was in shock and awestruck.

How could this event have happened? Why did this poor fellow get stopped in his tracks right in my doorway and frozen like a statue?

I knew instantly why. When the roommate came to his senses he looked at me and asked how I could be so calm and stand there and smile when some guy just had a knife pulled on me. It was easy. Jesus had just done for me what I could not ever have done for myself. You see, an hour before this crazy incident I had plead "The Blood of Jesus" over my little home and myself, my roommate and my dog, just one hour before the outsider showed up.

I still have a picture in my mind of that scene of my roommate, my dog and me, trying to get our minds around what had happened. But it was real. Real, real!

The power of God to protect and defend us had just been demonstrated in a way that could not be denied. Thank-you Jesus! God had given me strength and peace and taken away all fear.

The "Blood of Jesus Prayer" is real. This prayer works. This prayer is powerful.

The big lesson is that when covered by the Blood, YOU NEED NOT FEAR.

The Scriptural Grounds for Pleading the Blood of Jesus

The bible has a large amount to say about the power of the Blood of our Lord Jesus Christ.

Many Christian churches and their pastors ignore this fact however. This is probably due to the fact that direct instructions are not given to us in the bible on how to use it. It is a body of knowledge that has been revealed over many centuries, however and today is a firm foundational teaching in many Christian churches.

There are numerous verses and lessons in the bible that teach us about the power of the Blood. What it means and what it can accomplish when understood and used by a true believer.

Christians recognize that the Blood was shed for our forgiveness. Solid bible believing churches teach that. Without the shedding of the Blood there would be no grace or forgiveness. Being covered by the Blood is our most powerful form of protection.

1 John 1:7 The Blood of Jesus cleanses you from all sin and guilt

Matthew 26:28 For this is My Blood of the new covenant, which is shed for many for the remission of sins.

Ephesians 2:13 But now in Christ Jesus you who were once afar off are made near by the blood of Christ.

It is only because of the power of the Blood that we can be forgiven, redeemed and receive eternal salvation.

But the bible has a lot more to say.

The Bible tells us that Jesus also defeated Satan and all of the powers of darkness when He served as the sacrifice for us, our sins and our souls. When Jesus was crucified, shed His Blood and resurrected, He did it all. He had to shed His Blood. He had to die for us. And through His resurrection He gave us the promise of the best gift of all-Eternal Life!

Hebrews 2:14 Since then the children have partaken of flesh and blood, He also Himself likewise partook of the same; that through death He might destroy him who had the power of death (that is, the Devil),

Colossians 1:13 For He has delivered us from the power of darkness and has translated us into the kingdom of His dear Son;

1 John 3:8 He who practices sin is of the Devil, for the Devil sins from the beginning. For this purpose the Son of God was revealed, that He might undo the works of the Devil

Revelation 12:11 And they overcame him because of the blood of the Lamb, and because of the word of their testimony......

Everything that happened on that day of our Lord's crucifixion was real and carried lessons for those in attendance and for us today. Jesus defeated the power of Satan on that day. The shedding of His Blood defeated death for all born again believers and it also defeated the dark powers and principalities of this world. The dark powers then and now. What Jesus did was for all generations. We acknowledge that power every time we take communion.

And they overcame him by the Blood of the Lamb

Who is him? It's Satan, and all of his minions (demons). Yes, all the demons and powers of sin have and can be defeated by the power of the Blood. Jesus' death was a physical one and it was the most important act of spiritual sacrifice for all man-kind that God provided for us

Jesus' death physically happened 2000 years ago and in doing so it fulfilled many prophesies out of the Old Testament. The shedding of the Blood of the Lamb was the most important act of protection for the Israelites. Likewise, the Blood serves as our protection and source of power today. As the spirit of death passed over the Jews on

Passover, supernaturally, so do the powers of darkness get defeated by the power of the Blood to this very day.

The bible lessons are all there and when these bible truths are expressed properly today, miracles again can and do happen

Jesus did it all. But we are all human. He was both fully man and fully God. We still have our sin nature to overcome. And only because of the Blood sacrifice of Jesus can we be empowered to Overcome it all, especially our fears.

The only missing link for many of us is to fully realize this incredible fact. We need to get a hold of this truth and not to be afraid to use it. We need to put our fear and timidity aside and rise up. Rise up and start using all the available gifts that the Lord has provided for us. Especially when the powers of darkness, the demons and evil people, are taking aim at us and doing their best to destroy us and our walk with the Lord.

The Word tells us that we have been given the power to dominate ALL darkness in this world, praise God! The bible tells us many times that we can and will be Overcomers of ALL, if we submit to the Lord's teachings and His ways

This bible verse teaches us an important truth.

Luke 9:1 And He called His twelve disciples together and gave them power and authority over all demons.....

Notice in this verse, that Jesus gives the twelve apostles power over all demons, not just some of them. That means that He has given us the power and authority to defeat the enemy in all their manifestations. Whether, the demonic is working through other people, places or things. All means All and in God's world there are no exceptions.

If we have God's power available to us to defeat all demons, then I believe that we have God's power to defeat any and all evil people who the demonic may be using to come against us, with any type of unjust or unrighteous action or attack. He has given us the authority to conquer all evil that tries to come into our lives. We need not be victims

Because of The Blood, we have been given access to all of this spiritual power anytime we are in need. God is always on duty and the Holy Spirit doesn't sleep. The power is always with us, where ever we are.

2 Chronicles 16:9 For the eyes of Jehovah run to and fro in all the whole earth to show Himself strong on behalf of those whose heart is perfect toward Him

The power that God has given each born again believer, through the Blood, is breathe taking to those new to this teaching. And for those who know God's powers, it remains one of the greatest blessings we have. The power that we have within us to overcome the enemy is one of the least understood facets of our faith. The problem with many Christians is they have not been taught the truth Then if taught, many don't believe. How sad.

If you are in one of those groups and are still full of questions or uncertainty, relax. You don't have to 100% believe or understand what is happening when you use this prayer. Go ahead and test it. You won't be testing God; you will be testing this teaching.

During these troubled times, we do not have to live in fear.

We can choose God for the answers to all our problems.

Brothers and Sisters, are you on your feet rejoicing? Hallelujah!!!

Jesus loves you so much.

These teachings are especially for these Days of The End, in which we live.

Lesson Eight

Putting it all into Action

CONGRATULATIONS! This is the last lesson in the foundational spiritual warfare teaching series from The Joseph Plan.

It is my hope and prayer that it has been rewarding for you. We have covered a lot of material. Much of it you will be able to put into use immediately. Some of it will become the building blocks upon which you can build your faith and relationship with our Lord Jesus Christ and the Holy Spirit. Over the last seven lessons you have taken a giant step. You have reached out and sought after answers that so many within the body of Christ don't even know exist. There are so many of our brothers and sisters that haven't been taught enough to understand that there is a problem, much less the answer.

This teaching series was not designed to be all inclusive or a doctorate level teaching. It was not written, nor was it intended to be an, everything you ever wanted to know course on the ways to defeat the devil and all the spiritual forces that work for him. But it was not an elementary level course either. We got into some very important foundational teachings, like the biblical roots for "Pleading the Blood of Jesus". That is one foundational teaching that you will be able to carry with you for the rest of your days. I felt it was necessary to be thorough in that particular core learning. You can go back to your textbook as often as you need for the rest of the story. It will always be there as a reference book for further study. Or to refer back to when you are ready to take another step in your learning. The sooner you start using these prayer techniques, the quicker it will be working for you.

Pleading the Blood of Yeshua on yourself and your family and your loved ones multiple times a day, should become a part of your everyday prayer routine. It is the most powerful prayer of protection that you can say. The stories that come into the ministry about this prayer never cease to amaze me. We serve such a wonderful and powerful God. Jesus truly loves each and every one of us. He wants nothing but the very best for us. He loves us so much that He was willing to suffer, shed His Blood and die for the sake of taking the curse of our sins away from us.

We learned how to "Plead the Blood" and other defensive prayers so we can live our lives free of fear and other spiritual attacks and be assured that "through Him" we have a protection in our lives that is truly supernatural. This is a supernatural protection that the rest of the world can only just dream about it.

The following few pages were taken from my second spiritual warfare book, "Break the Bondage of Fear". It addresses the need to trust in the Lord enough to actually use the teachings you have been given, even when things become a little uncomfortable or possibly dangerous.

*** Chapter 8-- Wouldn't it be great if there was a way to live free of fear (read demonic oppression) and any other spiritual bondage that you had become free of? Wouldn't it be wonderful if there was a way we could be assured that we were not going to be drawn back into the type of thinking and life style that invites the enemy's attacks?

It is one thing to break free from all the demonic strongholds, like fear, that had put one in chains. It is quite another to be able to look forward to each new day with the confidence that the demonic is not going to raise its ugly head and ensnare us once again. Well, there is a way and you have already been shown it! Our assurance rests in our Lords loving and protective hands. He never wavers in His love for you.

We may need to learn how to talk to the Lord again or for the first time and re-learn how to pray.

The answer is living your life in a faith that trusts our Lord Jesus Christ, trusting In Him enough, to know absolutely, that He is going to protect you. He will do that for you. He already guides and protects millions of us from the evil one each and every day. There is no reason you are an exception to His love. He NEVER EVER discriminates in His love for us. When we are saved and filled with the Holy Spirit we receive everything from Him that we will need to live a life free of fear and other spiritual dark powers. Walking with the Holy Spirit and trusting in Him we can, indeed, live every day free of the Bondage of Fear. You don't have to return to that place ever again. You are now reborn or born again and are walking with the spirit of God within you. You are now spiritually adopted into the family of believers, just like a child is adopted into a new family. You are now what the bible refers to as a "Son (or daughter) of God". And along with your new adoption papers comes a new authority.

As you are probably aware of, Jesus, as God, has spiritual authority over all of His creation. He can take authority and cause the entire natural world to move. But He is still allowing us to live with our free will as He has done for 6000 years. And all this authority has been given to each and every born again Christian. Do you have any idea how much of a force we could be if the entire body of Christ were taught about the Lord's authority and how to live with it?

This teaching on the authority of Jesus Christ is one of the most needed and least taught by mainline Christian denominational churches everywhere. It is such a shame.

Countless numbers haven't been taught that the Word of God, through His Spirit, renews and can lift our spirit over the evil deeds of the devil and all his evil helpers.

There are celebrities and fad philosophies that claim to hold the keys to being able to "Break the Chains of Fear and other demonic powers" and claim to hold the secret to "Becoming free of all your Bondages". These claims I am citing are not anyone's title to a book. But they all suggest worldly answers to our spiritual problems. If one can't find a self-help book that satisfies them, just wait a month. Another popular advice book will be released. There are, however, books giving good Bible based teaching and I encourage you to use whatever the Lord leads you to learn from. As we have shown, the Bible is our source for this knowledge and the Holy Spirit is our primary guide and our power.

There is only one authority that you can call on "every time" to protect you, that will always be there for you and will never change. And that authority is God. God, the Father. God, the Son and God, the Holy Spirit. God has authority over all of creation and because He now dwells "inside you", He continues too through you. God's Word shows us examples of how to be transformed and to make a decision to turn our lives and bodies over to God. We do not need to take the fallen worlds style and standards, which allows evil to run our lives. Open your eyes and fill your heart and mind with God's loving plan for your life.

You can be an Overcomer.

The following is a story about what happened to my wife and me in 2012. It demonstrates well the principle we are dealing with here. This is a true story of a Diamondback Rattle Snake that came knocking at our door.

It was my first experience with a Diamondback Snake and it was a real big one, at least in my world.

Most of us have heard about the dreaded Diamondback Rattlesnake. It is very poisonous, for those of you that aren't familiar, and can be very undependable. In fact it is one of the most poisonous snakes in the SW United States. In late 2012 I had my first experience with one. Having lived in Arizona for almost fifteen years I have heard many stories and have seen them in zoo's and only a couple dead ones on the road. I had seen a few baby rattlers here and there, but I had not come face to face with a full grown one. That day I was in my office writing. Kate saw the cat watching something outside and beginning to get agitated. Kate went over to the door and was stunned.

Right outside our door was a 4 1/2 foot Diamondback snake, which was hissing and rattling at the cat, through the screen door.

Kate yelled-"Thomas-Come here - quickly!!!! Thomas!!!!! Get out here!!!! Help!!! Please!!!

I bounded out of my chair- (suspecting an issue or a little trouble of some kind) and came out to find my wife looking out of the front door, pointing. Pointing at this snake that the cat had been so worked up over. It was a coiled rattle snake about six inches from the door. And it was a monster, at least in my world, and it didn't seem very friendly.

I grew up in the mid-west US and we did not have many poisonous critters, snakes or otherwise. I did not have a reservoir of experience to draw upon.

So I proceeded to go out to protect my girls, with no clue of what to do. As I stepped out of the door, I moved very slowly. The snake was wriggled to the left and off of the sidewalk. This was a big snake and the famous rattles were sounding the alarm.

Now here's the scene. I'm standing outside facing off with this snake. Kate and a neighbor were yelling at me. Saying things like "don't get too close, you'll get killed". Or, "Thomas, he's moving towards you-RUN!"

So I did the best thing I knew. I got my lawn chair out and sat down to study the situation. I honestly didn't have a clue. The snake was far enough away that I wasn't in mortal danger. Then I said a short prayer. When I called on the Lord the spirit was poured out and it came to my mind to plead the Blood. I said a prayer for the Lord's protection as promised in Psalm 91 and plead the Blood of Jesus on the situation.

That snake was coiled, with her head reaching up and hissing. With a leg that barely works and only being off my cane for a few months, I didn't feel like much of a match. So I quietly called on the One with all the power. When I called on the name of Jesus and plead "the Blood of Jesus" prayer" for protection, the snake responded by moving over next to the house and coiling up. Every time she would move towards me I would toss a few pebbles her way to get her attention, put my hand up and command her to move away and "Be Still". She obeyed directly each time. Frankly, I didn't know if I should be surprised or scared, because I had never been in this position before.

This went on for about an hour and a half. She'd raise her head and wriggle toward me, flash her tongue and I'd command her to "In the name of Jesus, Be still", "Go back." She would pull back and coil up each and every time. I was really winging it here, trying to follow the lead of the Spirit.

We had called the fire department and explained the situation when this drama had first started. They took the report and said they would try and get someone over to help. They know that I am disabled and not very agile on my feet. The dispatcher understood that it was best for me to not to try and capture this beast on my own. So we waited and waited.

For almost two hours we waited and about every five, ten or fifteen minutes that snake would rear up and start coming my way and it would get commanded to move back. Each time it retreated back next to the building. When the fire department finally arrived all was under control. The fireman just walked over with a long handled snake tool and put her into a bag. They then escorted her back out into the desert.

It was just me in my chair with a cup of coffee and Jesus keeping watch over this Diamondback snake.

Under the authority of Jesus Christ and out of the mouth of a believer, All of Creation must obey.

With God's help I am now a man with experience in dealing with the great southwest viper!

It is a cute story with a big lesson for all of us. Don't hesitate to try it on something harmless. Please understand. That was a story about the power of the Holy Spirit, not me. In the presence of God, that snake had no choice. God's will was obviously at play here. I was always prepared to get out of that snakes way, if the situation demanded it. But trusting in what I believed and saw the Spirit of God doing.

When we are a baptized, born again, spirit filled believer, we are automatically under the authority of our Lord Jesus Christ and we have "the authority" to say:

"Under the authority of Jesus Christ and through the power of the Holy Ghost, I Plead the Blood of Jesus upon myself and my family for protection and care". (Protection from _____ and the care of _____.) AND

"Under the authority of Jesus Christ and through the power of the Holy Ghost, I rebuke, bind, break the spirit of Fear (or any other spirit) and command you to come out of _____ NOW in the name of Yeshua, my Lord Jesus Christ"! Thank-you Jesus. Amen.

Or, "I rebuke you, Oh worker of Satan, in the name of Jesus Christ"

Or, "Under the authority of Jesus Christ, I command xxxx (you) to come out ____."

When proclaimed, the spirits of darkness, all evil spirits, must obey, they have no choice. They all must obey under the authority of Jesus Christ. Only He is the highest in the heavens. Even Michael must worship Him. The Holy Spirit of God has spoken through you when you are speaking IN Authority. God/Jesus is more powerful than any fallen spirit. They were once angels until they revolted against God and made the decision to follow Lucifer. Fallen angels are demons.

But it is important that we are prepared for the battles of the natural fallen world that come upon us. If you want a life that is free of worldly Fear and demonic attacks or influence, God has provided us with the tools, the Word and prayers.

You can live each day with Free of Demonic Oppression.

You are being given the keys to the Kingdom for living free.

By learning to be in submission to Him and His ways in all humility and walking each day in obedience. The Spirit of God is your guide.

Living and operating under the authority of Jesus Christ, through the power of the Holy Spirit, should be a goal of every born again, spirit filled Christian. It is the ultimate of An Enduring Faith, which we are all going to need during these "last days" that we live in. You know in your soul that this is true as we watch people of the world rising up in anger and shuttering in fear.

1John 4:4 you are of God, little children, and you have overcome them, because He who is in you is greater than he who is in the world.

Who is Jesus talking to here? He is talking to His children, all those who are saved and assured their salvation through Him.

There is misinformation and non- biblical teachings in many churches today. We have to know- that we know- that we are assured salvation and an eternal heavenly place with Christ. When we are given that gift and the understanding of what it means, we then KNOW! We will know with confidence.

How does one know they are saved for sure? We will know because, with His assurance we will be able to operate under His authority and able to perform deliverance. (Did you get that?)

We will know that we know Jesus Christ and are walking with the Spirit of God:

When we- are in Christ by keeping His word (1 John 2:5)

When- the love of God has truly been perfected in us by keeping Christ's word (1 John 2:5)

When at- the last hour, because antichrist is coming and many antichrists have appeared, we will have discernment (1 John 2:18)

When-everyone who hates his brother is a murderer - you know that no murderer has eternal life (1 John 3:15)

When-He who knows God listens to the Scriptures, he who is not from God will not, By this we know the spirit of truth and the spirit of error. (1 John 4:6)

When-We know we abide in God because He gave us His Holy Spirit (1 John 4:13)

When-We are assured that we have eternal life (1 John 5:13)

Do you know Jesus? Does He know you? You probably know absolutely by now.

When we are assured of our salvation--We just know! We aren't necessarily perfect, but we know perfectly, that we are one of His kids. We have been adopted into His family.

There is only one way to know and be assured- Ask our Father in heaven in Jesus Christ's' name in prayer today.

Rom 8:16 The Spirit Himself bears witness with our spirit that we are the children of God.

When we ask the Lord, in Jesus Christ's name, He assures us with His peace and understanding. If for any reason you question your salvation, go to a quiet place, alone, and talk to Jesus. Repent of your sins and commit your life to Him. Then go to a bible believing church and get baptized. Ask for an anointing from God that will stir your spirit.

Yes, when we know, that we know, that we know---WE DO INDEED KNOW. His Grace is strong enough to cover all sins and we are nor the exception. We know that we are Sons and daughters of God and that no man can take that away from us.

Bonus Lesson

Self Deliverance

Spiritual Warfare Training on Self Deliverance.

ARE YOU SUFFERING from the effects of the evil one in your life?

Are you under spiritual attack and suffering from nightmares, strange thoughts or odd occurrences or disease in your life?

Do you need Deliverance from Evil thoughts, actions, voices or diseases affecting you?

Do you need to be delivered from the torments of Satan and his workers? Are you under demonic attack and in need of finding PEACE?

You are about to learn how the power of God can change lives forever!

God wants us living free of the effects of the demonic and provides us with the tools. One of the promises and free gifts of Jesus is that we can be delivered from any influence the enemy has in our lives! We can find freedom from all sin and the demonic through Jesus Christ. Through Christ there is an answer and no born again Christian is an exception.

All born again Christians have natural enemies. Satan and his army of demons are at war with all of us. It is the duty of all born again Christians to be armed and ready to conduct the battle with the enemies of God through Spiritual Warfare and Deliverance.

Eph 6:10 Finally, my brethren, be strong in the Lord, and in the power of his might

Eph 6:11 Put on the whole armour of God, that ye may be able to stand against the wiles of the devil

Eph 6:12 For we wrestle not against flesh and blood, but against principalities, against powers, against the rulers of the darkness of this world, against spiritual wickedness in high places.

God has given every born again Christian the spiritual tools or armaments to be victorious in this battle.

Remember the saying that possession is nine tenths of the law. That is a general rule of law in society. In spiritual warfare possession *is 100%* of the law. Regardless of our spiritual condition, if we leave the demonic free to operate in just one part of our life; we are giving the devil legal permission to operate within our lives! Because, in spite of our good intentions, the devil has a stronghold.

A stronghold is a base of operations for the demonic. It is a house of wrong thinking, a fortress of bad thoughts or ideas. We get them from our natural self, our parents, society and from bad teachers.

A stronghold of sin occurs when our thinking develops a sinful bad habit, attitude or a belief that is contrary to God's will and Word. Through our thinking or non-thinking we give that sinful habit, situation or attitude permission to be present in our life. Once we accept sin as part of who we are we have given the demonic permission to operate from their new stronghold in us. The evil one has established a base of operation.

2Co 10:3 For though walking about in flesh, we do not war according to flesh.

2Co 10:4 For the weapons of our warfare are not fleshly, but mighty through God to the pulling down of strongholds

,2Co 10:5 pulling down imaginations and every high thing that exalts itself against the knowledge of God, and bringing into captivity every thought into the obedience of Christ;

2Co 10:6 and having readiness to avenge all disobedience, when your obedience is fulfilled.

The roots of most stronghold's are based in sin. Unrepentant Sin! One of the gifts that God gives us, when we are born again, is the ability to be delivered from the spiritual strongholds of sin. When a "born again believer" repents of this sin, the Holy Spirit has the power to remove the spirit that has been using the stronghold that the sin created. But one must be born again.

Spiritual Warfare and Deliverance must be used to become free of many of them.

God has given each born again Christian the weapons to conduct this battle, the battle that we must fight on a daily basis. It is a personal battle that requires close contact fighting and a battle that most of us must fight from within. It is a spiritual battle that we have to overcome, a battle that will be won when it is brought to the strongholds in our lives from which the demonic operates.

All spiritual battles require spiritual warfare.

Spiritual Warfare can be used to conquer the enemy outside of ourselves or spiritual warfare against the strongholds the enemy has within us. The Joseph Plan deals with spiritual warfare with the enemy outside of us and/or within other people, in other teachings onsite.

In this teaching on Deliverance we are going to concentrate on overcoming and winning the battle within, the battle that the enemy is waging against our very soul. This teaching is on Self Deliverance!

Remember that the goal of the enemy, Satan and his hordes of demons are to ruin our testimony and relationship with Jesus. They want us living in sin, full of mis-teachings, sick, mentally disturbed or dead. The enemy will always try to bring upon us what is bad or evil, never anything that is truly good for us in God's world. Oh, he may use deception to give us temporary pleasure, but the goal is always evil. The evil ones plans for us are always the opposite of God's. Whether easily discerned or not.

Becoming free of the enemy "within us" is called Deliverance, being delivered from the hold the demonic has on us and our lives. It is the act of a believer moving from a state of oppression or disease, to one of freedom and good health IN Christ.

It is the process of helping ourselves to claim the victory that Christ died to give us is called Deliverance! The purpose of deliverance is to set free any born again Christian who is in bondage to any of the wiles of Satan. (Which is many, unfortunately.) Many of us seek the help of a Christian Deliverance minister, which we recommend, when we discover we are in need. But when there is not one available, we can acquire the tools to do Self Deliverance.

It doesn't matter what you call the bondage (demonized, possessed, oppressed, insane etc.), if one is in demonic bondage, whether they need to tear down a stronghold, break up a legal ground, cast out a demon, or all three, it is still called deliverance, because through it we are setting the captive free. Casting out demons or the demonic, is just part of the deliverance process.

This act or process to free oneself of demonic oppression is called "Self Deliverance"!

All born again Christians are called to do Deliverance. Do you believe the Word of God? The methodology for this lesson was provided by our friend Michael Smith of Hardcore Christianity, which is located in Phoenix Arizona.

Mar 6:7 And he called unto him the twelve, and began to send them forth by two and two; and gave them power over unclean spirits;

Mat 10:8 Heal the sick, cleanse the lepers, raise the dead, cast out devils: freely ye have received, freely give.

Luke 10:17 And the seventy returned again with joy, saying, Lord, even the devils are subject unto us through thy name.

Luke 10:18 And he said unto them, I beheld Satan as lightning fall from heaven.

Luke 10:19 Behold, I give unto you power to tread on serpents and scorpions, and over all the power of the enemy: and nothing shall by any means hurt you.

Luke 10:20 Notwithstanding in this rejoice not, that the spirits are subject unto you; but rather rejoice, because your names are written in heaven

Yes, if you are a saved, born again and spirit filled Christian, you already have the POWER to do Self Deliverance. But I do caution you with this biblical principle.

Mat 18:20 *For where two or three are gathered together in my name, there am I in the midst of them.*

In tough cases, Deliverance can be accomplished best when done by a trained prayer group or by an experienced Deliverance Minister.

Can a Christian be demon "possessed? NO!

To be possessed means that the evil spirits are living in your spirit and are in control of the person. The Holy Ghost lives in the spirit-man & the demons cannot get into this area.

Can a Christian have demons or be "demonized? YES!

The Greek word "daimonizomai" is translated as "possessed" in the KJV. It means to be under the control of a spirit, in whole or mostly.

Demons can enter INTO the body or the brain of a Christian in many different ways.

A) They may inhabit the body or brain prior to salvation & were never cast out after being born again. I call this "CARRYOVER" (see Teaching section).

B) They may have entered the body or brain when the Christian backslid & turned their back on the Lord to return to a sinful lifestyle.

C) They may have entered the body while in the womb thru a family or word curse. The person may be "oppressed" & the demons may not be INSIDE the body or the brain. They may be attacking from the outside only.

Does it say anywhere in the Bible that a Christian CANNOT have a demon? NO!

Teaching that a Christian cannot have demons is an "old wives' tale" and a false teaching. Jesus called deliverance "the

Children's Bread" (Mt. 15:26). Deliverance is for God's children. It was paid for in the Atonement. Delivering sinners or all non born again Christians from demons is dangerous, because they have no spiritual weapons to fight the spirits off when they attempt re-entry. If the spirits re-enter the body the person's condition can worsen (Mt. 12).

Can a Christian be SELF-DELIVERED from demons, physical diseases & mental illnesses? YES!

The ministry of "Laying on of Hands" applies to all believers, including oneself (Mk. 16:18). Because Jesus said: They shall take up serpents; and if they drink any deadly thing, it shall not hurt them; they shall lay hands on the sick, and they shall recover. Do you believe that? Just because it isn't among one's life experiences, doesn't mean it isn't true.

Can a Christian have a demon that oppresses them and affects their thoughts and actions? Yes, yes, yes!

The traditional, denominational teaching is that a Christian cannot have a demon. That is total silliness. Christians can sin and Christians can have demon or two, etc.

Sin of any kind in our life gives the demonic legal authority to operate in an individual. Compare this to someone owning one lot in a development of 200 homes. The demonic can gain access of one of the houses and cause major oppression, thus spoiling the desirability or value of the entire community. The host community is now oppressed, because of one of its parts. The demonic took possession of one part and caused problems for or oppressed the whole.

A Christian can be tempted into sinful thoughts or actions. That sinful action, if left unrepentant, will give the demonic legal permission to act out its evil ways. That one unrepentant sin can spoil or ruin the testimony of the entire person or make them sick, but it does not mean that they are "possessed" as the world use the term.

The Apostle Paul had a Demon and if he could have one so can you or I. 2Co 12:7 And lest I should be exalted above measure through the abundance of the revelations, there was given to me a thorn in the flesh, the messenger of Satan to buffet me, lest I should be exalted above measure.

There are two qualifications for Deliverance.

Every person must meet these qualifications before being delivered.

First, you must be a saved, born again Christian.

That means a Christian who, as an adult, has repented of all of their sins and turned their will and their life over to the care of Jesus Christ. The Jesus Christ of the Holy Bible. Not the Jesus of the Book of Mormon, the Jesus of the Koran and not the Jesus of Rick Warrens "Purpose Driven Life". These three are "bloodless" and not true biblical portrayals of Jesus Christ. We must have made a real decision.

Secondly, You Must Be WILLING.

That is right, you must be willing. Willing to do whatever it takes to acquire the freedom offered by the true Jesus Christ. You need to desperately want to change. There are no alternatives. You need to desperately want the enemy defeated and removed from your life. A CASUAL APPROACH WILL NOT WORK! If you hold back, the enemy, the evil spirits will sense your hesitation and they won't leave. God gives us free will and we need to make a clear decision that He can and will defeat the enemy within us. We go to Christ in faith asking for a complete victory over the enemy in our lives.So, if you are a saved, born again Christian, I invite you to volunteer for the battle. It is one you can win. Are you willing?

Self Deliverance Plan of Action

Be ye Warned! IF YOU HAVE NOT REPENTED OF ANY SIN IN YOUR LIFE AND NOT FORGIVEN EVERYONE IN YOUR LIFE WHO HAS HARMED YOU and/or YOU ARE NOT WILLING TO MAKE RESTITUTION FOR ANY OF YOUR WRONG DOINGS, WHEREVER APPLICABLE, YOU SHOULD NOT PROCEED! God has set up rules for those entering into this battle and having a repentant heart is a core one.

That is the foundation of which your personal relationship with God is built and it is absolutely necessary before actually doing Deliverance. Please pray about this with great sincerity and be very honest with yourself. There may be negative consequences in proceeding, if you aren't sure and the odds of your deliverance being successful will greatly diminish. Your temptation will be to jump right in and go for the solution to your troubles. I encourage you to slow down and try to be very methodical about this. Don't do as so many of us do and skip some parts. Every word and line on this page is there on purpose. Slow down and prayerfully proceed.

If you have any questions about this, I invite you to do a salvation check here. There is only One who is the source of all forgiveness! When we repent we are truly changed and the power of the Blood washes us clean.

You must be ready to fight for your life. Are you willing to go into a battle to get well? The Kingdom of God suffers violence & the violent must take it by force

Mat. 11:12 And from the days of John the Baptist until now the kingdom of heaven suffereth violence, and the violent take it by force.

If you won't fight, the demons won't ever be evicted. They don't respond to please and thank-you, nice guy approaches.

When you are ready, spend as much time in prayer as you can prior to the deliverance time you have set and ask a couple of close friends to pray for you in preparation. Keep fasting to a minimum. Get plenty of rest. You must show the Lord and the Kingdom of Darkness you are serious. If you don't show them, they will continue to show you; sickness, misery, suffering, sorrow, frustration, disease and heartache.

IF so, Praise Jesus, let's get on with it. Let's start by making formal preparations for this spiritual battle.

Mar 16:17 *And these signs shall follow them that believe; In my name shall they cast out devils;*

The gifts given us by Jesus did not stop two thousand years ago.

As a born again Christian you already have the power to cast all evil out of your life. Your battle is not with flesh and blood.

Eph 6:12 For we wrestle not against flesh and blood, but against principalities, against powers, against the rulers of the darkness of this world, against spiritual wickedness in high places.

Ephesians chapter six has been a teaching of many Christian denominations. You are probably already familiar with it. In it there are four important things we are to learn about our enemy. Our battle is not with flesh and blood, but with:

1. Principalities

2. Powers

3. Rulers of Darkness

4. Spiritual Wickedness in high places

Those four define who we are in this battle against. All are spiritual.

• The first mentioned is Principalities. The Greek word for principalities is archas. This word is used to describe a series or ranks that make one power more powerful than another. An example would be a military rank. Satan is the head of the dark kingdom. His army is divided into different ranks. All having different authorities and powers.

• Powers is the second term used. Powers in the Greek is *dunamis*. Our word dynamite comes from this Greek word. The inference is that God will give the Christian explosive power that is much greater than the enemy.

Act 1:8 But ye shall receive power, after that the Holy Ghost is come upon you:

All the power you will need to overcome the enemy in your Deliverance will be supplied by the Holy Ghost or Spirit. This enhanced power comes to the believer through baptism and anointing by the Holy Spirit.

• We wrestle with the Rulers of the Darkness of this world. The Greek word for Rulers or world leaders is kosmokratoras. Translated- "Lords of the world"!

Through the authority and power of applying "The Blood of Jesus" you are going to be an overcomer!Here are some good powerful verses from Scripture showing that all Christians now have God's supernatural power and anointing available to them, so they can use it to engage with the dark side of this life:

"Behold, I give you the authority to trample on serpents and scorpions, and over all the power of the enemy, and nothing shall by any means hurt you." (Luke 10:19)

Notice in this verse we have God's power over all the power of our enemies, not just against some or part of their powers. This means we have the ability to come out completely victorious in some of life's battles and struggles, but only if we learn how to properly use what is now available to us.

"Then He called His twelve disciples together and gave them power and authority over all demons, and to cure diseases. He sent them to preach the kingdom of God and to heal the sick." (Luke 9:1)

Notice in this verse that Jesus gives the twelve apostles power over all demons, not just some of them. As you can see from the way all of the above Scripture verses are worded – true Christianity is not a weak, wimpy, or passive religion. As born-again believers, we all have the Holy Spirit literally living on the inside of us. As a result, our bodies have now become the actual temple of the Holy Spirit. His supernatural power is now fully available to all of us in order to help us handle some of the storm clouds that can come against us in this life.

Learning how to "Plead the Blood of Jesus" for deliverance and protection is the primary armament in our arsenal for

Deliverance. The spiritual world is very organized. It is structured like a highly disciplined military unit. It has an order of authority and it is divided into specialties of service. Each spirit or demon has very specific roles and tasks they are assigned to do.

If you decide to conduct Self Deliverance, you are going to have to take spiritual dominion over and conquer all of the above mentioned entities.

But first let's take a look at some of the more common reasons for someone needing Deliverance. Each of the following represents different spiritual entities. You will gain an understanding of your enemy by studying this list.

Your knowledge and ability to take dominion over the demonic forces controlling each of the symptoms listed will be enhanced as you gain in knowledge about what they are. For this we can use:

1. – Discernment. Asking the Holy Spirit to explain and provide the answer.

2. – Detection. Doing the footwork and research to discover which demons are at work in your particular case.

There is a very extensive list of demonic entities in my book entitled the "Biblical Spiritual Warfare Manual". But you may be able to have a successful Self Deliverance by simply calling on "all the demonic entities involved in causing xxxx symptom". It will be worth your time to do some homework on this and try to identify, as close as possible, the controlling demonic forces that have the power behind your issue or symptoms. Calling Out the "Spirit of Lies", for example, will often work. A trained and experienced Deliverance minister will have a heightened discernment on this matter.

Common Symptoms for the need of Deliverance.

Each of which is associated with a particular demon or family of demons. Refer to the list of known Demons in your manual for the associations.

1- Sudden outburst of Anger

2- Sudden outbursts of Rage

3- Realizing unjustified Fear

4- Thoughts of harming oneself or others

5- Outbursts of misguided Emotions

6- A different personality appears regularly

7- Hearing voices often

8- Weird or "anti" thoughts come to mind

9- Unclean thoughts concerning sex

10- Harmful or uncontrolled use of the tongue

11- Paralyzed by Anxiety or Depression

12- Involvement in any Occult, Spiritualism or a New Age False Religion

13- All Phobias

14- Extreme Obsessive or Compulsive behavior

15- Confused or disorderly thinking

16- Attraction to false religious doctrines

17- Most diseases that can only be treated and not cured by modern medicine

18- Any disease that fails to be healed by competent medical treatment

19- Lack of sympathy with another's pain or need.

20- Absence of righteous anger or other God given emotions

21- Excessive risk taking

22- Lack of zest and enthusiasm: listlessness, sadness, mood habitually down

23- When there is no regret or remorse when involved in sinful activities

24- Controlling Addictions of any kind

25- Outbursts of violence and Hatred

26- Inability to follow a plan or order of things

27- Inferiority complex – feelings of worthlessness

28- Substantial weight gain or loss

29- Too much or too little sleep habits

30- A series of physical ailments which do not run a typical course and/or fail to respond to treatment

31- Extreme insensitivity or unkindness to others or animals

32- Loss of or lack of a sense of Humor

33- Excessive Risk Taking

34- When someone is easily Deceived

35- When easily discernible lies, are often accepted as Truths

You may have one, two or many of the above listed. Write them down and do some research about them. All the above symptoms can be overcome by the "Blood of Jesus" through Deliverance! The Lord may add or subtract from this partial list.

Self Deliverance Procedure: (I recommend you look up and study each of the bible verses and ask the Lord to put them upon your heart.)

1 Worship the Lord & tell Him how beautiful & wonderful He is. Invite the manifest presence of the Holy Spirit into your room. Relax while worshiping. Take your time. Express your love for Him & your complete dependence on Him and His mercy (Ps. 150).

2 Lay down in a comfortable spot in a quiet & dimly lit room, void of auditory or visual distractions. Relax and meditate on the goodness of the Lord & His Word. Reduce your heart & breathing rates (Ps. 46:10, 63:6).

3 Place your hands on the skin of your lower abdomen and silently, in your mind, begin to cover yourself by faith with the precious Blood of Jesus Christ thru your groin, hips and internal organs. Worship, glorify and magnify His Greatness and thank Him for His Blood as intensely as you can. Meditate on the rich, beauty of His life saving Blood. Pray in your mind only, not audibly (Mk. 16:18, Mt. 19:15).

4 Repeat this procedure over your stomach, heart, throat, forehead and the back of the neck. Spend several minutes on each area, silently praying/meditating on the precious, powerful, healing, delivering, enriching, Blood of Jesus as sincerely and as aggressively as you can (Mt. 8:3). These are the areas spirits usually reside.

5 You may start to feel something unusual begin to occur in your body such as: twitching, pushing, pulling, pressure, tightness, butterflies, quivering, shaking, aching, coldness, cramping, paralysis, nausea or subtle internal movements. Give yourself permission to throw up if necessary. You may have strange thoughts racing thru your mind. These are spirits manifesting. These sensations indicate you have the Anointing of the Holy Spirit, the demons are in revolt and moving in fear. The Holy Spirit's presence, through the power of The Blood is exposing and defeating the hold of

the spirits. Push and keep going! Your faith is working! This is evidence that God is working during your Deliverance and is winning.

6 If you experience violent shaking, severe cramping, frightening visions, loud voices or have material objects move in the room, DISCONTINUE your prayer time & seek assistance with someone you trust who has experience expelling evil spirits (Mk. 9:20). Some devils simply need the prayers and authority of trained Deliverance ministers or teams.

The spirits of lies and deception should be addressed at the beginning of your Self Deliverance. Always put all Lying Spirits and Deceiving Spirits under "The Blood of Jesus" when you first start a session.

***If you are having serious thoughts of self harm or suicide, I strongly recommend that you call your doctor or emergency services immediately. Then after medical treatment you can commence with Self Deliverance.

Expelling the Evil Entities:

1 Demons are subject to the Name and Authority of Jesus under the "Blood of Jesus", The Cross and Resurrection of Christ, the Word of God, the Holy Ghost and your child like Faith. Christ came in the flesh. Jesus IS Fully God! He shed His Blood for you.

2 Speak directly to the spirits (Mk. 11) and your physical or mental illness & command them to leave your body & mind in the name of and by the authority of Jesus Christ. You are not praying anymore. You have already prayed and God said yes. Take command and use your authority, the authority you were given by Christ through His Blood sacrifice (Lk.

10:19, Mt. 18:18). Remind the demons that you have repented of all your sins, that all doors to sin have been closed and that they have no legal right to damage or hold you in bondage anymore. If God gives you the name of the demons or their number, you can use this information to command them to leave as Jesus did in Mark 5:8-9. You can also call them out by the symptoms they are causing (disability, depression, pain, lust, anger, envy, confusion, fear, cancer, bipolar, ulcer, OCD, PTSD, etc.) as Jesus did in Mark 9:25. The important thing to remember is that the Holy Spirit, through the power of "The Blood of Jesus" is strong enough to take total command. The demonic has no choice at this point. They MUST OBEY! Sometimes easily and sometimes after a great battle, but they have no choice. Jesus Wins! Believe and be victorious!!

3 Remind them that the Lord Jesus came to destroy their works & the devil is defeated (Jn. 12:31, 16:11). Command them to listen & leave. You have been given power to crush serpents and scorpions & over ALL the authority of the enemy (Lk. 10:19). You will not be hurt. Continue to tell the devil about the Blood and how they are defeated & command them ALL to leave your body & brain in the mighty name of Christ Jesus. Command them to "Get Out"! "Get Out"! In the name of Jesus Christ I command you to "Be Loosed and Get Out" right Now.

4 When the spirits leave, you may experience something physical: pressure lifting off your head or body, dissipating coldness, coughing, vomiting, burping, spiting, yawning, wrenching in the stomach or shaking & releasing. When they leave you may feel a euphoria, body warmth or lightness come over your brain or body or a clearing in your mind. This is a sign the spirits are leaving or have left your

body. Keep going. You are winning in Jesus mighty name.Rebuke them sharply, strongly & bind them up (with strong spiritual cords, if necessary.) and command them to loose their hold on you (Mt. 18:18). Cast them out of your body and mind and into the pit of Hell.

"Under the authority of Jesus Christ and the BLOOD of JESUS that He shed and the Power of the Holy Ghost, I bind all familiar and unfamiliar spirits, including the spirits of (fill in the blank) and (name of the spirits or the symptoms), I loose their hold on my body and mind, and I Break them and Cast them out. I command them to leave me, this room and this house NOW and cast them or send them to the pit of hell. "Go! Go! I command you to Get Out! You have NO authority here. You have lost your power and your entire claim to me and xxxxx." "I now Plead the Blood of Jesus upon "my symptom and/or name of the demons hold", for cleansing, healing and care. The Power of the Blood of the One Living God cannot be denied!

Thank-you Jesus! Thank-you Father! Thank-you Holy Spirit. You are the only ONE who has the Love and Power to do this for me.(Feel free to repeat the above as many times as you feel is necessary. You aren't being tested on this. Hallelujah!) Freedom will come!

Demons can be "beaten down" by Godly commands & Holy Scripture. Once you start, be persistent and command them into submission. They have lost their authority and their days are done. They'll figure it out that they are now defeated. Quote Bible verses about the power of the Blood and the Glory of the Cross. We provide many in the teaching entitled: How to Plead and Pray the Blood of Jesus, which can be found in the below link. I highly recommend you study it before commencing with

Deliverance. *http://thejosephplan.org/how-to-plead-and-pray-the-blood-of-jesus-prayer-spiritual-warfare/* (A Must Read)

The power of pleading "the Blood of Jesus" by a born again, spirit filled Christian is undeniable. I strongly encourage you to study it intensely. I have written a book on Spiritual Warfare that includes an extensive teaching on this vital topic, called the "Biblical Spiritual Warfare Manual". It is available in our donation based book store onsite and at Amazon. You can examine it here.

5 Renounce any spirits that got into your body thru religion or church denominations (Catholicism, false protestant churches, Mormonism, Christian Science, Advent-ism, JW's, Hindu, Islam, Buddhism, Masons, Shriner's, KKK, cults, etc.). Renounce all sexual obsessions or perversions (adultery, fornication, escorts, group sex, divorce, bestiality, sexual abuse, pornography, etc.) & sinful friends & the occult (palm readers, horoscopes, readings, channeling, talking to the dead, astrology, religious rituals, tarot cards, etc.). Renounce anything satanic. Renounce any spirits that entered your body thru sexual intercourse (hetero or homosexual) with someone who was infected with them. That book also deals with how to break "curses" that may have been brought to you through your own sin, your family of origin or by evil people.

6 After you are delivered, repeat this entire teaching again. Go thru the entire "Procedure" section again to be sure they are all gone. If they are not, repeat steps 3 & 4 again. If they have all left, spend the next hour worshiping the Lord & immediately seek the Baptism of the Holy Spirit (Rom. 8, Acts 2, 8, 10, 19, I Cor. 14). This is critical! Don't skip this

part. It is the Holy Spirit that is going to seal your Deliverance.

VERY, VERY IMPORTANT! Please, please complete this Bible study right away: Acts 19, Romans 12:1-2, I John 2:15-17, Eph. 4: 21-32, 6:11-18, II Cor. 7:1, John 5:14, 8:11, Matthew 12, Luke 11, Heb. 12:1, Jas. 1:21, I Thess. 4:7. If you skip this part you may be leaving the door open for the demonic to return seven times more powerful into you. Take the time, it's your life.

Praise Jesus! The above teaching has been used by Christians all over the globe to rid themselves of the workings of evil one and his hordes of minions.If you completed your deliverance and would like to share your experience about the power and life changing authority of God, please write the ministry a letter. We would love to hear from you.Write- *breakthebondage@thejosephplan.org*

It is my hope that that this training has been a total blessing to you and all those close to you.

May God Bless you and keep you Safe,

Pastor Thomas Holm

The World Wide Ministry of The Joseph Plan

www.thejosephplan.org

I give a big Thank-you to Brother Michael Smith of Hardcore Christianity in Phoenix, Arizona for contributing to this teaching on self deliverance. Meet his Deliverance Ministry at: *www.hardcorechristianity.com*

About the Author

Rev/Pastor Thomas Holm

THOMAS HOLM IS THE MINISTER/PASTOR of The Joseph Plan and author of "Break the Bondage of Fear" and the "Biblical Spiritual Warfare Manual".

Christian ordained minister, seasoned recovery and care pastor, author and researcher. Age 64 in 2014.

Thomas and his wife Kate live in a small town in the eastern mountains of Arizona. (for the peace and quiet)

Thomas has served in Christian ministry since 1998 in Arizona. He served the Lord first as a recovery, trauma and Care minister and Christian pastoral consular. An "on the street" minister and bible teacher. He was then moved by the Lord to evangelism and an outreach ministry called Third Step, which was formed in 2003 and reached hundreds of thousands of the lost for Christ over the next eight years. The Joseph Plan was called and formed in 2011 and continues today. It has served hundreds of thousands. He has never served as a head pastor in a church, his experience is in the real world and all of its oppressions and battles of life.

Since his first vision from the Lord in 1998, Thomas' ministry has encompassed spiritual warfare. The Lord put the right men in his path starting back in 1994. Through their guidance he studied and learned. He learned one step at a time, from local and internationally renowned spiritual warfare ministry teachers. Jim Miller of Mesa, Arizona and Jim Searcy of Cyprus were very instrumental in his learning's.

Pastor Henry Gruver has been and continues to be a major influence.

Thomas believes that one of the biggest shortcomings of today's Christian church community is its lack of spiritual warfare teachings and that every Christian NEEDS to be taught it. Not just for today's battles, but because of the days of the end that we live. The demonic is rising and so should we to be an Overcomer!

Thomas is available for guest teachings, pulpit replacement and appearances at your church or conference by special arraignment. You may contact him at: *BreaktheBondage@thejosephplan.org*

This completes the Spiritual Warfare training course from The Joseph Plan. It is my prayer that you have stepped up and grown with it.

I encourage you to go slow. This teaching is just the beginning of your growth. Try to discuss what you have learned with other Christians. Talk to your pastor. Maybe He or She would like to get the congregation involved in a church wide training. Try to bring these teachings into a small group for discussion and practice.

It has been a joy for me to serve as your teacher for this short teaching. If you have been half as blessed as I have during this process, it is a total win-win. Praise Jeshua. Thank-you Jesus. You get all the praise.

The World Wide Ministry of The Joseph Plan

If you write to ask about possible scheduling please put "appearance" in the subject line.

Rev/Pastor Thomas is available to bring this teaching series, through multimedia presentations, instruction and group discussions to the right groups.

I may be contacted at: *ministry@thejosephplan.org*

Psalms 91

God Bless and may He keep you Safe!

Thomas

Made in the USA
Lexington, KY
12 November 2015